OFFICIAL

RIVEN™

THE SEQUEL TO MYST®

HINTS AND SOLUTIONS

by William H. Keith, Jr. and Nina Barton

BradyGAMES
STRATEGY GUIDES

LEGAL STUFF

Riven™ The Sequel to Myst® Official Hints and Solutions

Brady Publishing
An Imprint of
Macmillan Computer Publishing USA
201 West 103rd Street
Indianapolis, Indiana 46290
ISBN: 1-56686-751-7

Library of Congress Catalog #: 97-070249

Printing Code: The rightmost double-digit number is the year of the book's printing; the rightmost single-digit number is the number of the book's printing. For example, 97-1 shows that the first printing of the book occurred in 1997.

99 98 97   3 2 1

Manufactured in the United States of America.

Riven™ The Sequel to Myst® Official Hints and Solutions

TABLE OF CONTENTS

Author Bios

William H. Keith, Jr.

As of this writing, Bill has written over 50 books and has several more in the pipeline, novels ranging from military technothrillers to military science fiction to science fiction comedy. Current series include Warstrider, an SF series under his own name, and SEALs: The Warrior Breed, a military historical-fiction series under the pseudonym H. Jay Riker. Before he started writing for a living, he was a professional SF illustrator and still occasionally exhibits his work at various cons and on the World Wide Web.

When he's not writing—]is there such a time?—he can be found hiking, blowing holes in paper targets with firearms of various calibers, participating in Western Pennsylvania Mensa events, and hanging out with some very strange people. He lives in the mountains of western Pennsylvania with his wife, Nina.

Nina Barton

After years of editing Bill's prolific output, Nina Barton—alias Nina Keith—has begun writing on her own, probably out of sheer self defense. Unlike Bill, she understands both computers and computer people, a highly desirable talent when working on a computer game guide for BradyGAMES.

She is currently co-writing several novels with Bill. When she's able to pry herself away from the computer, she likes to hike, go to concerts, teach piano, shoot things, go to Mensa conventions, and hang around in bookstores. She lives with Bill in western Pennsylvania.

This is Bill and Nina's fourth book for BradyGAMES.

Author Acknolwedgements

Any game guide like this one is of necessity a collaborative effort by many people. We would like to extend our special thanks, however, to Tim Cox, our editor at BradyGAMES, and to Brady's Acquisitions Editor Debra McBride, who made it all both possible and worthwhile.

Of course, there would be no game guide without the game, or the talented team of programmers and developers who put it together, but we would like to especially thank our guides through Cyan's land of Riven, Robyn Miller, Rich Watson, and Bonnie Staub.

And finally, our very special and sincere thanks to Cyan's Chris Brandkamp, who opened to us the mystical and wonderful universe that is Riven.

BRADY STAFF

Publisher
Lynn Zingraf

Editor In Chief
H. Leigh Davis

Licensing Manager
David Waybright

Marketing Manager
Janet Cadoff

Acquisitions Editor
Debra McBride

CREDITS

Project Editor
Tim Cox

Screenshot Editor
Michael Owen

Book Designer
Carol Stamile

Production Designers
Phil Pierle
Tina Trettin

CHAPTER ONE
Introduction

"Sunlight dances off an azure sea. You hear the cry of wheeling gulls overhead, the buzz and click of insects in the verdant forest growth. You stand alone on the rocky shore of an island where, in the distance, you see strange and wonderful devices luring you forward with the promise of mystery and wonder. It has been long since you unlocked the puzzles of Myst Island and freed Atrus from the prison of dark and labyrinthine D'ni. A new test and new challenges await you now.

Welcome to the Fifth Age and the mysterious world of Riven.

Riven is a complex and challenging game, replete with puzzles of devious and almost diabolical cunning. Riven The Sequel to Myst Official Hints and Solutions is designed to enable you to work your way through each location within the Fifth Age and make decisions for yourself. Do I want a word or two to push me in the right direction? Or, do I want a step-by-step listing of the places I must go and the things I must do to crack each puzzle in turn?

Vague to Specific: How Much Do You Want To Know?

Each chapter of this book is rated according to how little or how much it actually gives away. To understand the graphic symbols that warn of spoilers to the game, however, you'll need to take a quick look at a few of the creatures that inhabit the islands of Riven.

The Beetle

This is a small and harmless creature you may see flying around in the jungle or crawling on a log.

A beetle at the head of a chapter means that *very little* is given away in that section. There are no hints or solutions of any kind, although some of the background information may be generally useful in your quest.

The Frog

You may or may not see a frog in your wanderings. Frogs are harmless, but they're a step up on the food chain from beetles.

A frog at the head of a chapter means that the section in question does contain hints, although no solutions are given away outright. Refer to these sections for subtle hints or a gentle nudge in the right direction.

The Sunner

You may, if you're lucky, encounter sunners in *Riven*. Sunners are bizarre, otherworldly creatures that resemble improbable hybrids of penguins, baleen whales, and plesiosaurs. Sunners are decidedly larger than frogs and much more mysterious.

A Sunner indicates that the section gives away quite a bit. It will stop short of telling you the solutions to the puzzles outright, but it *will* take you to the very brink of revelation. If you'd rather figure out the puzzles for yourself, don't look in these chapters!

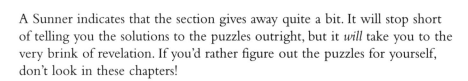

The Wahrk

You may never encounter one in your travels, but signs of the wahrk's existence —and its importance to the world-islands of *Riven*—are everywhere. It is an aquatic beast, a melding of whale and shark, and it is undeniably dangerous.

The wahrk icon is reserved for those sections that give away *everything*. If you want to preserve any of the mystery and brain-teasing wonder of *Riven* and you come to this symbol, do not read any further!

CHAPTER BY CHAPTER
The Book of Riven: Hints and Solutions

Now that you've completed your lesson in *Riven* zoology, let's look at how the chapters of this book are organized.

CHAPTER ONE: Introduction

This introduction to the game and the book gives away nothing of substance. It includes this description of the book's chapters and a section on how to use this book.

CHAPTER TWO: Roaming Through Riven

This is a brief chapter that, again, gives away very little. It provides a quick look at the game controls and cursor types, and a brief overview of how to maneuver through the worlds of *Riven*.

CHAPTER THREE: The Islands of Riven: Hints and Musings

This chapter is divided into seven sections, one for each of seven places you can visit in the course of your travels. Each section begins with a brief description of the place, followed by lists of hints and tips (arranged top to bottom) that range from vague to specific. The solutions to puzzles and problems are *not* given away outright, however. You still have to work for some things!

CHAPTER FOUR: The Islands of Riven: Maps and Specifics

As in Chapter 3, this chapter is divided into sections describing each area within *Riven*. This time, however, each area is mapped out in detail; for

example, looking at a map of Jungle Island will definitely give away some of the surprises, if only because you will know what's on the other side of that tunnel or which direction on a forking path to choose in order to reach a particular control. Also included are lists of the puzzles and problems that must be solved in order for you to proceed through the game, along with some specific hints and tips for solving them.

Use this chapter carefully if you want to preserve the mystery and suspense of the rest of the game!

CHAPTER FIVE: Walking Trough the Fifth Age

This chapter, presented as a journal, provides a walkthrough of the entire game as described by one explorer. Be aware, however, that one person's experiences (the order in which he solves the puzzles, the particular directions he explores, the choices he makes) will almost certainly be different from yours! Use this chapter as a guide, both to the atmosphere of *Riven* and to the logical processes, the lines of thought you must pursue, in order to arrive at the right conclusions.

This chapter *does not* reveal the solutions to any of the puzzles outright, but it *will* suggest courses of action and thought that will reveal quite a lot. Don't look in this chapter unless you don't mind having much of the mystery and surprise revealed!

CHAPTER SIX: Puzzles and Problems: The Solutions

The Gate Room. The Gallows. The Star Fissure Window. This chapter lists each of the major puzzles and problems in the game and tells you how to solve them. Remember, though, that much of the pleasure of playing *Riven* comes from piecing together the subtle and widely scattered clues that enable you to reason out the answers for yourself. *Please* don't look in this chapter unless you're totally baffled and cannot solve the problem in any other way!

CHAPTER SEVEN: Walkthrough: All Revealed

This is the spoiler chapter, the one that gives away *everything*. It takes you step-by-step through the entire game, solving each puzzle and showing you exactly what to do to get from the beginning to the end, assuming no missed steps and virtual clairvoyance on the part of the player. At the end of the chapter, you will find brief descriptions of the several alternate endings to the *Riven* saga.

Walkthrough: All Revealed will actually prove to be most useful to you after you've completed the game, because it will help you piece together everything and see how it all works and how you might have done things differently. Do *not* read this chapter if you want a chance to work things out for yourself!

APPENDIX A: How It All Came To Be

This relatively brief narrative, gleaned from the journals and dialogues of the various characters in *Riven*, provides a detailed look at the backstory of *Riven*. It details who constructed what, and why and what it has to do with the story line of the game. This appendix *does not* give any specific puzzle solutions, but it does assume that you have completed the game and know all of the secrets, which it may refer to in passing. If you would rather learn about some important revelations in the game as you play, don't read this section.

APPENDIX B: Worlds for the Making

Did you know that merely observing something might be necessary for that something's very existence? That describing a world—or a universe—might actually call it into being? A brief essay on the bizarre and real (whatever *that* means!) world of quantum mechanics, on the multiplicity of alternate universes, and on the probable realities of *Riven*. This section refers to specific locations and personalities within the game only in passing and gives away nothing important.

Using *The Book of Riven: Hints and Solutions*

Perhaps you've just purchased *Riven* and are wondering how to start. More likely, you've played through the game until you encountered a deviously twisted puzzle which, after hours of play, thought, and head-scratching, you cannot solve. Or, possibly, you've only heard about *Riven* and are reading this book to get an idea as to whether you really want to lose yourself in this fascinating, alternate reality.

Wherever you're coming from, *you* decide how much you want the writers of this book to tell you. Read the section in this chapter entitled "Vague to

Specific: How Much Do You Want To Know?" to learn about the four sym-bols that represent the "level of spoiler" provided by each chapter.

If all you want is a general overview of the game mechanics (what the different cursors are and how to move around) read Chapter 2, "Roaming Through Riven." There are also some very general suggestions regarding gameplay, or things to keep in mind as you move from to place to place.

You're stuck, but you don't want us to tell you the answer. If all you want are some gentle hints, check out Chapter 3, "The Islands of Riven: Hints and Musings." The hints are arranged by location, puzzle, or problem, from top to bottom, ranging from vague to more specific and direct. You might want to use an index card to cover up the hints that appear farther down each list, which will enable you to reveal each hint one at a time without giving away more than you want to know.

Even with all of our carefully worded hints, the twisted cunning of a partic-ular puzzle or set of clues is just too much. What you need is straight talk about how to solve a particular problem, but without having the answer handed to you on a platter. If you want to see maps of the various locations, or would like a list of the puzzles and problems you must solve in each loca-tion with some hints on how to go about it, read Chapter 4, "The Islands of Riven: Maps and Specifics." If you would like to read a journal entry walkthrough that conveys some of the mystery and atmosphere of the game along with a description of the logic behind the puzzle solutions, try Chapter 5, "Walking Through the Fifth Age." If you would prefer to read a narrative about Riven's backstory, which describes what the different loca-tions and puzzles mean and what they're all about, read Appendix A, "How It All Came To Be."

Okay, okay! Enough hints, vague suggestions, and cute stuff! If you read the words "Have you checked the entire room carefully for clues?" just one more time, you're going to commit cybercide! You're up against a steel-plated wall, and there is *no* way you're going to solve this puzzle in any time less than a decade or two.

If you want the specific solutions to each of *Riven*'s puzzles and step-by-step revelations describing how each problem can be solved, read Chapter 6, "Puzzles and Problems: The Solutions." If you would rather see a walk-through that reveals everything, taking you from start to finish in the shortest possible time, go to Chapter 7, "Walkthrough: All Revealed." This chapter takes you through all of Riven by the most direct path possible, but be warned that you will lose most of the flavor and enjoyment of the game this way. Chapter 7 is best used *after* you've already successfully completed the game as a way of checking how well you did, or to see how else the game might have ended.

And finally, before you begin, here is one free piece of advice for playing Riven. Take your time! Enjoy and *savor* each location. Live it. Think about it. Turn it around in your mind. Take the time to puzzle each mystery out, rather than reaching for this book each time you face a problem that, at first glance, appears insoluble.

Riven is a universe of startling complexity, realism, consistency, and thought-fulness. Some of the problems are extraordinarily difficult, but you *can* work them out if you think them through. There are no time limits, but there is a universe of satisfaction that comes with each successful solution, each mastered clue, each correct assumption, each completed link.

Enjoy!

CHAPTER TWO
Roaming Through Riven

This is a BEETLE chapter. It gives away very little in the way of game secrets or solutions.

Unlike so many other CD-ROM games, Riven has a player interface that is simple, direct, and natural, almost as though you're physically in the world you are exploring. Getting around is literally a matter of pointing and clicking.

Notice the hand-shaped cursor on your screen? The appearance of the cursor changes depending on the actions that are available to you.

To Walk Forward

Move the pointing cursor to the spot on the path to which you want to go and then click. The view on your screen will change to reflect your changed point of view. Sometimes you will need to click on a particular part of the screen in order to move forward. Note that there will be times when it is simply not possible to move any farther. If clicking on the view ahead has no effect, turn left or right or try looking up or down to locate another route.

To Take a Left or Right Path

As you approach an intersection, you can choose which path to take by moving the forward cursor over the desired path and clicking. With sharp turns, you may need to move abreast of the intersection, turn, and then move forward as you normally would.

Turn Left/Right

Move the cursor to the left or right side of the screen until you see it point in the indicated direction. Click and your point of view will rotate 90 degrees.

Turn Around

In open spaces, turn left or right twice to turn yourself around and face back the way you came. In close quarters (for example, a cavern or a tunnel), the left- or right-pointing finger will appear crooked, as though pointing back over your shoulder. Clicking when you see this cursor appear turns you 180 degrees.

Look Up/Move Up

Move the cursor to the top of the screen. If the up-pointing hand changes from palm away from you to palm facing you, so that you can see the fingers, clicking the mouse will enable you to look or move in the direction in which the hand is pointing. Note that it is not always possible to look or move up.

Look Down/Move Down/Move Back

Move the cursor to the bottom of the screen. When the cursor changes to a down-pointing hand, clicking enables you to look down (over the edge of a cliff, for example), move down (descend a ladder), or move back (retreat from a close-up view). Note that these actions are not always possible.

Push/Pick Up/Handle/Manipulate

Keep an eye on your cursor. If there is something on your screen that can be manipulated (for example, a switch that can be thrown), you will see the icon change to an open hand. Click or click and drag to manipulate the object.

Zip

When the Zip feature is selected in the menu bar, the cursor may change into a small lightning bolt when it is moved to a particular area of the landscape. If you see the lightning bolt, you can zip directly to that location. This is a great time saver; it prevents a lot of trekking back and forth. Just remember that there's a lot to be learned from the landscape—don't miss it all in the rush!

The world of Riven is there for you to explore. Experiment! Try everything! You will very soon find that the cursor controls are second nature. Just remember: If something doesn't work, try something else. There has got to be a way to get to where you're going!

General Hints for Exploring Riven

This is a hint book, so the following are a few very general hints. These are things to keep in mind as you explore the complex, beautiful, and fascinating world of Riven.

Examine Everything

There are numerous objects in Riven that provide you with a closer look at items. Click on them to get a better view. Some devices enable you to further manipulate them by opening them or turning them on, which may prove to be important. Play with everything and note the results. Several devices have eyepieces, peepholes, or image viewing areas that require an up-close peek. Click on them to have a look.

Have a Look Around

The panoramas of the Riven sea and landscapes are breathtakingly spectacular. Stop frequently and take a careful look around. Admire the scenery, but also search for geographical clues. Try to orient yourself in the landscape, and be especially aware of the various buildings and structures and how they're sited on the various islands. You will need to pick up on such geographical clues as the location of certain bridges, where they lead to, whether they're open or closed, and so on.

If In Doubt, Turn It On

Try everything, throw every switch, pull every lever, and note the results. There are some mechanisms in Riven that must be set in a particular combination with other mechanisms, or which must be turned off so something else can be turned on. In general, it's in your best interests to turn on everything.

Understand the Mechanisms

You will encounter numerous mechanisms in Riven, strange devices that you must manipulate to open, move, look into, or turn on. Examine all such machines carefully by moving the cursor over them to check for areas that seem to allow you to manipulate them in some way. Then click and drag on the various controls. Try different combinations. Try to understand what the thing does and what it's used for. There may be subtle clues—a new sound or a change in some part of the landscape around you. Try to pick up on these clues and piece them together to form a picture of how the machine works and why.

Be Systematic

One lever may turn the power on or off for a number of locations, depending on how it is set. You may need to experiment by throwing the lever to one position, and then moving around and observing things to see what was turned on and what was turned off before returning and trying it in a different position.

Be Observant

Nothing in Riven was placed without a reason. Note such relatively minor details as where a steam pipe vanishes into the rock and try to determine where that same pipe emerges on the other side. Discover what it's connected to and you might figure out what it's for! Be aware, too, of the sounds you hear. A few will be important enough that you will want to take note of them, so that you can remember them later.

Be Persistent

Some puzzles may take many, many attempts before you crack it. Some will require you to travel back and forth between widely separated parts of an island, or even between several different islands, before you've assembled all of the necessary clues. You may notice something new about a scene each time you go there. Keep at it!

Read the Journals

Atrus gives you his journal at the beginning of the game. Later, you may be able to acquire or read the journals kept by Catherine and Gehn. Read them! They are not there solely as background or atmosphere. There may be specific clues—even codes or the solutions to specific puzzles—hidden within these pages.

Keep a Notebook

Don't trust your memory, especially if gameplay is going to extend over a period of weeks or months! During your explorations, you will be required to learn certain symbols and relate those symbols to other things. When you see a symbol that is obviously intended as something more than decoration, copy it down. You will probably need it later!

Make Maps

Veteran game players don't need the following advice: Make maps of your journeys, and note what you find at different points along the way. Chapter 4 of this guide includes maps of all of your destinations, but the thrill of discovery and the satisfaction of a deduction confirmed is much richer if you keep that chapter closed for the time being and draw your own maps as you explore. There are important clues in the relationships of certain structures, one with another, and the function of some controls can be inferred by noting the existence of pipe or walkway connections.

Keep a Journal

Atrus, Gehn, and Catherine all keep journals of their experiments, thoughts, and decisions. Shouldn't you? Some puzzle solutions require careful thought and the accumulation of clues from widely diverse locales. Many clues you acquire won't be needed until late in the game, when the larger picture finally begins to make sense. A journal of your thoughts, musings, and speculations might help you pick up on subtle, but necessary, clues.

Save Frequently

Here's another piece of advice that veteran gamers recognize: Save often! This adventure requires a lot of traveling to work out the various puzzles and problems. It would be a real shame if you were almost all the way through, and then discovered that you'd made a mistake or a rash assumption and had to return to the beginning to retrace your steps!

In general, save your game before traveling to another island or before getting too deeply involved in a new puzzle. That way, if things go wrong, you can restore your game from your last save, instead of repeating the whole thing.

Take Your Time!

Riven is an extraordinarily rich and complex world. You are under no time restraints and you are not in a race. Take your time and enjoy the experience! It may take you several gaming sessions to crack a particular puzzle, numerous restores from saved games, and many different approaches to find the right sequence or code.

And remember! If things get too impossible, well, that's why you have this guide book, isn't it?

CHAPTER THREE
The Islands of Riven: Hints and Musings

This chapter is designed to provide you with hints and clues to further your explorations of the world of Riven. It is divided into seven sections, five of which comprise the five islands of Riven, and two others for, well, call them "other places" for now. If you need help in a particular location or solving a problem, find the appropriate section and scan the headers until you find the list of clues you need.

The clues are arranged from top to bottom, from more general to more specific, so you might want to use a piece of paper or an index card to cover up the clues that appear lower on the list. Doing so will reveal only what you *want* to see, and not the entire solution.

This section is rated as FROG. It gives away some of the mystery and will certainly make some of Riven's puzzles easier to figure out. It *does not* expose specific solutions, however.

Temple Island

Temple Island is the place where you start your quest. There are a number of specific sites and machines located here, all of which are important to the game.

The Opening Drama

When you arrive, you're trapped in a cage. A man dressed in a dirty white uniform appears, carrying a knife or short sword in a scabbard. He tries to talk to you in an unknown language, and then grabs your Trap Book. A moment later, he slaps his neck as though stung, and then collapses, the victim of a blow-gun dart. Next, another man appears, his face masked. He takes the book, operates the lever that opens your cage, and smashes the cage mechanism.

> ▶ Does all of this tell you anything about the people of Riven?

> ▶ The first man wears a uniform, although it looks more like it is wearing him.

> ▶ Does that tell you anything about a local government or power structure?

> ▶ He's attacked by someone who moves cautiously, a guerrilla or rebel. What does that tell you about Rivenese society?

TIP: THERE'S NOTHING YOU CAN DO AT THIS POINT CONCERNING THE RIVENESE OR ABOUT GETTING YOUR TRAP BOOK BACK. STILL, YOU MUST BE AWARE OF RIVENESE CULTURE AND LIFE. GEHN FANCIES HIMSELF TO BE THE CREATOR OF THIS WORLD AND ITS PEOPLE. COULD THERE POSSIBLY BE *DISSENT* HERE?

The First Mechanism

When you are first released from the cage that imprisons you upon your arrival in Riven, you can see a mechanism of some sort—like a steel ice-cream cone—located just ahead.

▶ What might this be for?

▶ Carefully examine the structure and what it is built on.

▶ The controls don't work. You will have to go somewhere else to switch on the power.

▶ Does the pipe give you a hint as to where the power might come from?

▶ The device appears focused on a particular point. What is located at that point?

▶ Obviously, you will need some sort of code to open the cover.

▶ What is that on the face of the machine. An eyepiece? It almost looks like the eyepiece for some kind of strange microscope or telescope… a viewing instrument of some kind, certainly.

TIP: THIS SHOULD WARN YOU THAT NOT EVERYTHING IN RIVEN IS POWERED WHEN YOU FIND IT. YOU'LL BE LOOKING FOR A NUMBER OF VALVES OR SWITCHES TO GET THINGS RUNNING AGAIN WHILE YOU'RE HERE.

The Gate Room

Your first serious challenge upon arriving on Riven is the Gate Room, a five-sided chamber that rotates 72 degrees clockwise each time you press the button in the outside antechamber.

▶ Study the room and try to understand the geometry. You might want to draw a map.

▶ There are only two doors inside the Gate Room, but they can align with any of five outer gateways in various combinations, leading in various directions.

▶ Looking through the peephole each time the gate is closed will give you clues as to what is happening, and how the room is supposed to work.

▶ The room can access five different gateways. It can access only two at a time, because there are only two open doors within the revolving room.

▶ Reference the door you first came into Position 1. The other gateways can be identified as Positions 2, 3, 4, and 5, going clockwise around the room.

▶ When you first enter the Gate Room, the open doors are at 1 and 3. Access to Position 3 is blocked by a metal grate, which must be opened elsewhere.

▶ By rotating the room three times, you can align the open doors with Positions 1 and 4. Again, a metal grate blocks access to the doorway at 4.

▶ To get at a doorway *other* than 1, 3, and 4, obviously, you must find another way into the Gate Room. Either you'll have to come at 3 or 4 from the other side, looking for a way to open them, or you must find a way to reach either 2 or 5.

▶ Explore. Try to visualize the layout of the room and its surroundings. Where might Position 2 be in relation to the outside of the hill? Where might Position 5 be?

▶ Is there anything to suggest an approach to one of those positions?

▶ When you find access to another Gate position, you can rotate the room so you can enter from that position.

▶ Keep this 1-2-3-4-5 geometry in mind as you experiment with rotating the room. To get to one position, you may have to rotate the room several times, go somewhere else, and then rotate again to reach the desired configuration.

TIP: DURING YOUR EXPLORATIONS, LOOK FOR SWITCHES, LEVERS, AND VALVES THAT MIGHT FURTHER YOUR QUEST. YOU'LL NEED TO RAISE THOSE GRATES THAT BLOCK POSITIONS 3 AND 4 IN THE GATE ROOM, FOR ONE THING, AND YOU JUST MIGHT FIND SOME NECESSARY POWER CONTROLS!

The Great Golden Dome

This enormous dome looms high above Temple Island and appears to be an important site.

- ▶ Obviously, the way to reach the dome is through the Gate Room.

- ▶ You'll need to solve the Gate Room puzzle to enter the dome.

- ▶ After finding the way through the Gate Room to Position 3, you can cross the bridge and enter the dome.

- ▶ Explore every catwalk you can reach. Find steam valves that you can turn. Determine what the steam pipes are connected to.

- ▶ Note the lever inside the entrance to the dome—the power is off. Can you find out how to turn it on?

- ▶ What does the lever do?

- ▶ Note the gap in the catwalk inside the dome.

- ▶ That large wheel could be the control to connect the catwalks, but you can't reach it from here.

- ▶ Obviously, there's a way into the Golden Dome from someplace else. Keep this in mind as you explore further.

TIP: AS YOU CONTINUE YOUR EXPLORATIONS, TRY TO WORK OUT ROUGH MAPS OF WHAT YOU FIND. THE RELATIVE POSITIONS OF WHAT YOU SEE MAY HOLD IMPORTANT CLUES. THIS ALSO APPLIES TO OTHER ISLANDS YOU MIGHT SEE IN THE DISTANCE. IF YOU SEE A NEARBY ISLAND WITH BRIDGES OR OTHER STRUCTURES ON IT, TRY TO VISUALIZE ITS POSITION RELATIVE TO THE ISLAND YOU'RE NOW ON.

The Fire Marble Dome

The reason for the strange name will become obvious later on. Right now, you have to figure out how to open it.

▶ The dome is spinning rapidly and there appears to be no way to approach it. Do you notice anything interesting about the dome, something engraved on the surface?

▶ What is that device with the spinning, shuttered wheel that seems to be aimed at the spinning dome? How does it work?

▶ The device is a kinetoscope, a mechanism that can pick up separate images through a rotating shutter as they turn past the lens, enabling them to be viewed as a kind of motion picture.

▶ The push button on top of the device catches one "frame" of the movie, one of the passing symbols.

▶ Is there anything about the rotating symbols that suggests that one symbol is more important than the others?

▶ Can you click the button on the kinetoscope in order to catch that one, highlighted symbol?

▶ You got it! The dome is open. Inside is a dazzling, burnished, golden sphere—a giant, fiery marble, in fact. Can you make out what's inside the Fire Marble by looking through the glass port?

▶ What is the mechanism of sliders and button for? How does it work?

▶ You will need another code to operate this device.

▶ Where might such a code be found? Who constructed the dome, and for what possible purpose?

TIP: DON'T FORGET TO NOTE THE SYMBOL THAT OPENED THE DOME. YOU MIGHT NEED IT LATER.

The Temple and Its Environs

Across the bridge that leads from the main entrance of the Gate Room is what looks like a separate island at first glance, but which is, in fact, a peninsula nearly sundered from the main island by the sea. Sooner or later, your explorations will take you here.

▶ Examine the passageway carefully as you go down.

▶ What's behind that door?

▶ Explore everything carefully. Push the buttons, pull the levers, and note what does what.

▶ When you've explored all that you can in the first room, follow the main passageway further. What do you find?

▶ If the big door in the main Temple is closed, you will need to backtrack to find the control. Where might the room controls be?

▶ The large room at the end of the passageway is a Temple area. The smaller room higher up the passageway appears to be a projection room of some sort.

▶ Think of the "Great and Powerful Oz," and "that man behind the curtain." What does this setup tell you about the guy who runs this place?

▶ The main doorway to the Temple leads to some kind of conveyance. Where might that take you?

TIP: KNOW YOUR ENEMY. GEHN CREATED THIS PLACE. KEEP AN EYE OUT FOR CLUES TO THE PSYCHOLOGY OF THE MAN, SO THAT YOU CAN TAKE HIS MEASURE.

After solving the Gate Room, the Great Golden Dome, and the Temple Door, you are finished with Temple Island—at least for now.

Jungle Island

A brief examination of the control panel of the mag-lev tram car outside the Temple door should suffice to show how it works. Operating the car will carry you on a wild and exciting ride across the ocean to neighboring Jungle Island.

Eyes and Animals—The First Site

When you arrive on Jungle Island, carefully explore the area where the tram car docks.

▶ Can you find anything unusual near the tram?

▶ What does the eye shape do?

▶ Is there anything interesting or unusual about the eye?

▶ This is a tough one and quite subjective. Go partway up the steps, turn, and look back. Can you see anything unusual about the mouth of the tunnel?

▶ Can you make out an animal shape, one with the wooden eye positioned in the place where a real eye would be?

 **TIP:** AS ALWAYS, NOTE EVERYTHING YOU SEE AND HEAR. THERE ARE CLUES YOU'LL NEED, OFTEN QUITE SUBTLE ONES, EVERYWHERE.

Eyes and Animals—The Second Site

Follow the steps up, then down, and turn left at the T-intersection.

▶ Be observant. What do you see ahead?

▶ They're alive. Each time you move, they raise their heads, as if disturbed.

▶ You can leave the path and try to get closer. Can you sneak up on them without scaring them?

▶ How close can you get?

▶ If you move while their heads are up, you will frighten them off.

▶ Try to get close enough to hear one of them deliver a sharp, harsh bark.

▶ Explore the rest of the beach area. Is there anything else of interest?

▶ Can you find another painted, wooden eye?

▶ Is the eye associated with another animal-like shape of some kind?

▶ What is unusual about *this* eye? Make a note of what you see and hear.

 **TIP:** THINK ABOUT IT. WHO'S BEEN LEAVING THESE WOODEN EYES ALL OVER THE PLACE WITH THE CRYPTIC SILHOUETTES? GEHN? THAT HARDLY SEEMS LIKELY. REMEMBER THE ATTACK YOU WITNESSED WHEN YOU FIRST ARRIVED ON RIVEN. COULD SOME COVERT OR SECRET GROUP BE AT WORK HERE?

Eyes and Animals—The Third Site

Go back to the point where you left the path, and then turn left. Follow the path through the side of a mountain to emerge overlooking Village Lake.

▶ Carefully explore the raised platform and ladders. Do you see anything unusual?

▶ You should see what looks like a stone pool with an irregular bottom.

▶ Turn the petcock to the right. The water will create the silhouette of something, although it may be difficult to make out exactly what.

▶ Can you find another wooden eye?

▶ Make a note of what you see on the eye, what you hear when you turn it, and the shape of the silhouette that is revealed in the stone pool.

TIP: WHILE YOU'RE HERE, HAVE A LOOK AROUND AND SEE IF YOU CAN TELL WHAT YOUR NEXT OBJECTIVE SHOULD BE.

The Submarine

From the stone pool, you can look up and to the left and make out a strange, spherical craft made of iron. When you stare down into the shimmering waters of Village Lake, you can just make out what might be iron rails crossing the lake's bottom. Could there be a connection?

▶ Is that another ladder on the far side of the pool? Where does it lead?

▶ You've gone as far as you can at this end of the path, but remember this place. You might have a use for it later.

▶ You're going to need to find another way to reach the submarine.

▶ Follow the path back the way you came (past the lagoon and the Sunners basking on a rock, up the hill and over the top, and across the rope bridge.) Make your way to the wooden pier/walkway that's visible from the other side of Village Lake. Ahead, you should be able to see the village.

▶ From the stone pool at the other end of the path you could see the village beyond the submarine. Can you work out the relative positions of where you were and where the sub is now?

▶ At some point, you will need to start climbing ladders and crossing plank bridges. Eventually you will reach the submarine, coming to rest on a ledge that seems to be some sort of ceremonial center.

▶ There's a lever. What does it do?

▶ How can you reach the submarine *now*?

▶ You will need to retrace your steps again, all the way back and around, past the Sunner rock, past the stone pool, and down the ladders. Now you will find that the submarine is resting at the bottom of a hole in the water.

TIP: UNLESS YOU START CONSULTING CHAPTER 7 IN THIS BOOK REGULARLY, YOU'RE GOING TO BE DOING A LOT OF BACKTRACKING HERE! BUT DON'T WORRY—THAT'S PART OF THE FUN, PLUS IT'S A WAY OF BECOMING *VERY* FAMILIAR WITH THIS WORLD. HOWEVER, DON'T LET FAMILIARITY BLIND YOU TO THINGS YOU MIGHT NOT HAVE NOTICED YOUR FIRST TIME THROUGH!

The Submarine Circuit

It's not difficult to determine how the submarine works. You will have to do some mapping, though, to figure out where the lake bottom tracks take you, and how to get where you want to go.

▶ Can you relate the directions of the branching tracks with the layout of docks and piers you've seen so far on the surface?

▶ Can you get to all of the docks?

▶ Without a ladder from the docks, you're stuck inside the sub.

▶ Perhaps you need to find a control room of some sort.

▶ When you find the Control Room, two switches are up, three are down.

▶ Can you correlate that with the number of ladders you've seen up or down?

▶ What happens when you throw all of the switches?

TIP: MAPS WILL HELP WITH THIS ONE, ESPECIALLY IF YOU CAN LINK UP WHAT YOU SEE ON THE SURFACE WITH THE PROBABLE DIRECTIONS OF THE UNDERWATER RAILS.

The School Room

This seems to be where the Rivenese children are taught their letters and numbers. You might learn something useful here.

> ▶ Do any of the artifacts in the schoolroom tell you anything about Gehn's character, or about the life of the people living under his rule?

> ▶ What do you think the point of the Wahrk Hangman Toy is? Besides instilling psychological terror in children, that is.

> ▶ Play the game and study the symbols.

> ▶ Is there a relationship between these symbols and those you've seen elsewhere?

TIP: RIVENESE MATHEMATICS USES A BASE 5 NUMBERING SYSTEM. TRY TO LEARN ALL OF THE NUMBERS BETWEEN 1 AND 10, AND FIGURE OUT HOW THE SERIES OF 6 THROUGH 10 IS BUILT ON 1 THROUGH 5.

The Jungle Island Fire Marble Dome

Just figuring out how to get to the dome is a problem, although you can see it turning atop its pedestal of rock near the sullen glow of a magma-filled fissure.

> ▶ What structure is located near the dome?

> ▶ Might that have anything to do with reaching the dome?

> ▶ Actually, there are two ways to reach it. If you don't find the path during your first exploration of the island, you should be able to find a back way to it later.

TIP: AFTER FINDING YOUR WAY TO THE DOME, MAKE SURE YOU RECORD THE SYMBOL THAT OPENS IT IN THE KINETOSCOPE.

TAKE NOTE OF WHAT THE FIRE MARBLE DOME IS BUILT ON. YOU'LL NEED TO REMEMBER IT LATER.

Gehn's Elevated Throne

If you find your way to the Jungle Island Fire Marble Dome, you can reach this building, which is perched on a cliff high above Village Lake. Figuring out what the levers do is easy enough. Now that you're here, what should you do?

▶ The throne looks almost directly down on the Wahrk Gallows, a place of execution. This place must have something to do with the gallows and what occurs there.

▶ Have you tried reaching the Wahrk Gallows from the submarine yet?

▶ Were you able to get to the center of the gallows platform? Why not?

▶ Is there any reason to think you might want to explore in that direction?

▶ Does one of the levers by the throne solve your problem?

 **TIP:** REMEMBER THE INJUNCTION TO THROW EVERY LEVER AND TRY EVERY CONTROL.

The Fourth Eye

Three of the wooden eyes on Jungle Island are relatively easy to find, especially if you have this book in hand. The fourth eye is a bit tougher.

▶ Have you searched all of the island thoroughly?

▶ Do you remember how you went off the trail a bit, back by Sunner Rock?

▶ Might there be other places where you can leave the path?

▶ Have you attached any significance, as yet, to the giant metal daggers that are scattered about Riven?

▶ Those daggers were not left by Gehn.

▶ The daggers are associated with someone fighting *against* Gehn… someone leaving subtle clues to something else.

▶ Try searching the paths in the jungle. Watch for places where you can leave the path.

TIP: THE FOURTH EYE DOES NOT HAVE AN ANIMAL SHAPE ASSOCIATED WITH IT, AS THE FIRST THREE DID. CAN YOU IDENTIFY THE ANIMAL THIS EYE IS ASSOCIATED WITH FROM THE SOUND IT MAKES?

THINK ABOUT IT. ONE NUMBER HAS BEEN FIGURING LARGE IN YOUR DISCOVERIES THUS FAR. WHAT IS IT? HOW MANY WOODEN EYES—AND THE ANIMALS ASSOCIATED WITH THEM—MIGHT THERE BE ALL TOGETHER?

You are finished with Jungle Island when you've accomplished the following: You've found the wooden eyes and associated each with an animal and a symbol; you've learned what the symbols mean; you've found out how to reach the Fire Marble Dome; you've entered Gehn's Throne Tower; you've learned the secret of the Wahrk Gallows; and you've discovered a new gateway.

This may require several return visits to the island to uncover all of this. Keep at it!

Crater Island

You have several options for getting off Jungle Island, but let's assume that you find the logging-car ride from the clear-cut area near the jungle. This leads you—in wild and surrealistic fashion—along an underwater path to a neighboring island called Crater Island. In fact, you may have discovered this route by accident early in your explorations of Jungle Island, because all you need to do is follow a path to a tunnel, climb down, and push a lever.

The Central Power Valve
Nothing works until you switch the power valve located in the middle of the lake.

- ▶ How many pipes are there?

- ▶ One pipe is different from the others and seems to provide constant power to those facilities along the cliff in the distance.

- ▶ Three of the pipes go to different places and are powered in turn by moving the steam valve lever.

- ▶ Where do the three pipes lead?

TIP: EXPERIMENT. POWER UP ONE MACHINE AND CHECK OUT THE RESULTS.

The Boiler Puzzle

Although you arrive on a log chipper, the first structure you see on this island is a huge boiler, which reduces log chips to a kind of paste for making paper. You will have to figure out how this machine works to get anywhere on this island.

- ▶ Explore the beach as far as you can in all directions. Looks like a dead end, doesn't it?

- ▶ Is there anything about the boiler that suggests another exit?

- ▶ Can you get inside the boiler?

- ▶ Is the furnace on? Can you turn it off?

- ▶ Can you find a combination of settings that lets you get inside the tank?

- ▶ Can you reach the central tube and ladder?

- ▶ What happens when you raise the grate?

TIP: TO WALK ACROSS TO THE LADDER INSIDE THE TANK AND GO DOWN THE LADDER, THE GRATE MUST BE RAISED, THE TANK EMPTIED OF WATER, AND THE FURNACE TURNED OFF.

THE TUNNEL TAKES YOU ON A LONG, DARK CRAWL, FOL-
LOWED BY A LONG CLIMB UP A LADDER, AND DEPOSITS YOU
FROM A DRAINAGE PIPE HIGH UP ON THE MOUNTAIN. FROM
THERE, YOU'LL NEED TO FIND A PATH LEADING OVER THE
CREST AND DOWN TO A RAILED PLATFORM.

Catching Frogs

You reach the railed balcony and find the locked hatch that
opens to the ladder going back down to the beach. At least
you won't have to crawl back through that drainage pipe if
you need to go back to the power control in the lake again!
Now go through the double doors in the face of the cliff.

▶ Can you figure out how to work the trap apparatus?

▶ It's pretty easy. The spherical device that opens from
the top is a trap. The tiny pellets to the right are food.

▶ Depending on where you left the power setting in the lake, you may
need to go back and restore power to this facility.

▶ Try to catch a frog. Listen to its call.

▶ Match the frog's call in your mind with the eye you found on Jungle
Island, the one inside the frog silhouette in the rocks. Now, why do you
think Gehn might be trapping frogs?

▶ Did you miss anything on your way back to the double doors?

▶ There are other passageways here. Can you find them?

▶ Try closing the doors.

TIP: YOU MAY HAVE SEEN THIS PSYCHOLOGY OF DOOR
DESIGN IN ACTION BEFORE. DOORS THAT, WHEN THEY OPEN,
SEAL OFF *ANOTHER* DOOR. VERY ECONOMICAL IN TERMS OF
MOTION AND VERY *SNEAKY*...

The Crater Island Fire Marble Dome

Down the stairs to your left as you face the front doors is the chamber where the Fire Marble Dome for this island is hidden.

- ▶ Can you find where the kinetoscope is hidden?

- ▶ Can you find the lens, even if you can't see the machine?

- ▶ Where might the kinetoscope be hidden?

- ▶ How can you get there?

- ▶ Watch it! The architect is pulling the same trick on you that he pulled before!

TIP: WHILE YOU'RE IN THE FIRE MARBLE DOME CHAMBER ON CRATER ISLAND, LOOK UP. SEE THE HOLE IN THE CEILING THAT RESEMBLES A CRATER MOUTH? REMEMBER IT. YOU'LL NEED IT LATER.

Gehn's Laboratory

The front door to the lab is locked, as you'll find if you follow the path through the hidden door to the right of the double doors. How else might you get in?

- ▶ Explore the path revealed to the right of the double doors as you go out.

- ▶ Can you get into Gehn's lab this way?

- ▶ As you were on the walkway, did you hear a sound you've heard before? What did it sound like?

- ▶ What happens to the sound when you throw the lever?

- ▶ What have you just done?

▶ After throwing the lever, check the frog-trap station again. Is anything different?

▶ Can you climb into the ventilator shaft?

▶ Where does that take you?

TIP: ONCE YOU'RE INSIDE THE LAB, TAKE YOUR TIME AND CAREFULLY EXPLORE IT. THERE'S A LOT TO BE FOUND HERE, INCLUDING SOME INFORMATION THAT IS VITAL FOR THE SUCCESSFUL COMPLETION OF YOUR QUEST.

You are finished with Crater Island when you have accomplished the following: Traveled through the boiler to the double doors; solved the problem of the frog-catching apparatus, the fan, and the fan motor switch so that you can reach Gehn's laboratory; found the Fire Marble Dome; and lowered the drawbridge between Crater Island and the Great Golden Dome.

TIP: AFTER REACHING THE GOLDEN DOME FROM CRATER ISLAND, YOU MAY WANT TO GO THROUGH AND TO THE LEFT TO THE PLACE WHERE AN EXTENSION OF THE CATWALK HAS BEEN DRAWN BACK. TURN THE WHEEL TO COMPLETE THE CATWALK AND OPEN THE PATH ALL THE WAY BACK TO THE GATE ROOM.

AND WHILE YOU'RE AT IT, YOU MIGHT WANT TO PULL THE LEVER THAT RAISES THE BRIDGE FROM THE GATE ROOM TO A POINT SOMEWHERE ABOVE YOUR HEAD IN THE GOLDEN DOME. DOING SO NOW WILL SAVE YOU SOME DETOURS LATER ON.

FINALLY, NOW IS YOUR CHANCE TO FOLLOW THE CATWALK OUTSIDE THE DOME AROUND TO POSITION 4 OF THE GATE ROOM. THROW THE SWITCH TO OPEN THE DOOR THAT PREVENTED YOU FROM GOING TO THE OTHER SIDE.

You should now have three possible destinations. You can ride the logging car back to Jungle Island (by climbing the ladder near the chipper). You can follow the path past Gehn's lab back to the Great Golden Dome. (If, back when you were on Jungle Island before, you turned the lever to power up the western drawbridge, you should be able to operate it when you reach the control lever.) Or, you can take a mag-lev tram to a new island. We'll assume for now that you do the latter.

Plateau Island

This is where you collect some serious clues to the major puzzles that you'll need to solve to reach the end of your quest. Here you'll start putting together *all* the pieces.

The Plateau Map

If you've been paying attention, you'll recognize this as a map of Riven.

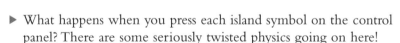

▶ Push each shape on the panel on the railing.

▶ What happens to the corresponding island?

▶ Can you correlate the islands on the Plateau Map with the island shapes on the control?

▶ What happens when you press each island symbol on the control panel? There are some seriously twisted physics going on here!

TIP: DID YOU REALIZE THAT THERE ARE *FIVE* RIVENESE ISLANDS IN ALL? THERE HAVE BEEN CLUES TO THIS FACT BEFORE (THE MAP/SIGN ON THE RAILING INSIDE THE FIRST DOOR YOU ENTERED IN THE GREAT GOLDEN DOME, FOR ONE) BUT THIS IS THE FIRST TIME IT'S ALL BEEN LAID OUT FOR YOU.

The Map Room Puzzle

Obviously, you're supposed to learn something here, although exactly what it is might have you scratching your head for a long time. It's clear that the plateau maps relate to these grid maps of Riven's five islands, and that clicking on each square brings up a 3-D relief map of that region. But why?

What are you supposed to do with this?

- ▶ At first, you might not be able to reach the Map Room. Have you checked the position overlooking the Plateau Map yet?

- ▶ Experiment. What happens in the Map Room when you press a button on the Plateau Map?

- ▶ What happens when you press one of the squares into which the island is divided?

- ▶ The creator of Riven did nothing without a purpose. There must have been something he was mapping on each of the five islands.

- ▶ What is the one specific significant artifact or construct that, so far, has been common to *every* island you've visited?

- ▶ Might there be a reason for mapping all such features of the islands?

- ▶ You must work out the map coordinates for each island map for the one feature common to all of the islands.

- ▶ The 3-D relief images are divided into 5-by-5 grids but are not otherwise identified. You must either draw maps of your own or invent your own grid system—something simple like A, B, C, D, and E across the top, and 1, 2, 3, 4, and 5 down the side. This would enable you, for example, to record the lower right square as "E-5."

- ▶ Examine each map segment carefully, sometimes from different angles, to ascertain the correct square.

- ▶ A clue to what you're looking for can be found if you consider the terrain near the Fire Marble Domes on Jungle Island, on Crater Island, and here on Plateau Island.

- ▶ On Jungle Island, the Fire Marble Dome rests on a cylindrical pillar of rock.

▶ On Plateau Island, the Fire Marble Dome rests just beyond a sharp, vertical cleft in the rock wall surrounding the lake.

▶ On Crater Island, the Fire Marble Dome was underground, but positioned directly under a crater or gap in the rock ceiling, open to the sky.

▶ These geographical features should reveal the positions of the Fire Marble Domes on these three islands with accuracy.

▶ Can you determine the position of the Fire Marble Dome on Temple Island?

▶ By this time, you will probably have visited four of the islands, but not the fifth. That means you'll have to take a guess concerning the location of the site there. Good thing it's a small island!

 **TIP:** BE VERY SURE TO COPY THE MAPS WITH THE DOME LOCATIONS OR RECORD THE COORDINATES. YOU WILL NEED THEM LATER!

The Lake and the Fire Marble Dome

The Map Room rests in the center of a crater lake. Another Fire Marble Dome is visible in the distance as it turns beyond a cleft in the rocks. There are some clues here that you will need in order to solve the Color Puzzle.

▶ What can you see in the lake, besides the Map Room building?

▶ How many of them are there?

▶ Can you distinguish different colors?

▶ The kinetoscope is broken and knocked out of alignment with the dome. It cannot be fixed.

▶ Can you stop the dome anyway?

▶ The problem of the broken kinetoscope can only be solved by a kind of brute force method.

TIP: TO STOP THE DOME ROTATION, YOU MUST CLICK THE BUTTON ON TOP OF THE KINETOSCOPE RAPIDLY (BASICALLY CLICK THE MOUSE AS FAST AS YOU CAN) AND TRY TO RANDOMLY CATCH THE RIGHT SYMBOL. THIS ACTUALLY WORKS FOR *ANY* OF THE FIRE MARBLE DOME KINETOSCOPES IF YOU HAVE TROUBLE CATCHING THE ONE CORRECT SYMBOL AS IT GOES PAST.

BECAUSE THE KINETOSCOPE IS BROKEN, YOU WILL NOT BE ABLE TO SEE THE FIRE MARBLE DOME'S SYMBOL THROUGH IT. YOU'LL HAVE TO LOOK CLOSELY AT THE DOME WHILE IT IS STILL CLOSED AND SPINNING (IF YOU'VE ALREADY OPENED IT, YOU WILL HAVE TO CLOSE IT AGAIN TO DO THIS) TO SEE IF YOU CAN IDENTIFY THE ONE YELLOW SYMBOL—OR AT LEAST NARROW DOWN THE POSSIBILITIES.

The Underwater Viewing Chamber

You may have to think for a moment about how to get from one side of the mag-lev tram car chamber to the other. Obviously, it must be possible to get over there; you can see a door on that side from the tram's cabin. But how to do it?

▶ The solution is obvious if you turn it around in your mind.

▶ When you get there, you'll go down a long, orange colored corridor. At some point, you'll see one of Gehn's scribes, who dashes off into a side chamber as soon as he sees you. Follow him and you'll arrive in time to see him getting into *another* tram car at a different station and whooshing off. You can't catch him, but remember this station, for later.

▶ Continue to follow the main passageway until you reach Gehn's Viewing Chamber.

Gehn's Viewing Chamber: The Color Wheel

▶ You have two devices to work with. What does each do?

▶ The device on the right has symbols on the dial. Do you recognize any of those symbols?

▶ What might the symbols refer to?

▶ Can you correlate the symbols with the color of the light shown in the display?

▶ The colored lights that switch on when you press the button match the colors painted on the wahrk totems you saw on the surface of the lake.

▶ You are looking for five colors, matched with five symbols. Unfortunately, there are six symbols in all, and—worse—one of the totems is missing and the light doesn't work.

 **FUN WITH WAHRKS:** THE RED LIGHT APPARENTLY CALLS IN A WAHRK FOR FEEDING. TRY SWITCHING ON THE RED LIGHT, LOOK UP, AND WATCH THE WAHRK APPROACH. IF YOU WANT TO MESS WITH THE WAHRK'S MIND, CALL HIM SEVERAL TIMES—EACH TIME YOU TURN ON THE LIGHT AND NO FOOD APPEARS, HE GETS TESTIER. THE FOURTH TIME HE SHOWS UP, HE GETS DOWN-RIGHT NASTY AND WON'T RETURN AGAIN UNTIL MUCH LATER.

Gehn's Viewing Chamber: The Viewing Screen

▶ The left-hand wheel has two buttons, which appear to show views from two different cameras. What do they appear to show?

▶ One shows a woman, alone in a room somewhere. Who might she be?

▶ Both Atrus's and Gehn's journals mention a woman. Where might she be?

▶ The other button shows several views of Village Lake on Jungle Island.

▶ The views on Jungle Island seem to be coming from the small island in the middle of the lake with what looks like a lens or camera on it.

▶ Do any of the images appear unusual?

▶ One image appears to be a silhouette of sorts.

▶ Have you been looking for a fifth animal silhouette?

▶ Can you spot something like an eye, tiny and indistinct, within the silhouette's outline?

TIP: YOU CANNOT REACH THE WOODEN EYE REVEALED IN THIS VIEW. KNOWING THE IMPORTANCE OF THE NUMBER FIVE, HOWEVER, YOU SHOULD BE ABLE TO GUESS WHAT NUMBER-SYMBOL IS CARVED ON THE BACK OF THAT EYE. YOU NOW HAVE THE INFORMATION NEEDED TO SOLVE THE PUZZLE OF THE 25 STONES.

You are done with Plateau Island when you have done the following: Figured out the Map Room Puzzle; found the Viewing Chamber; linked the various Fire Marble Dome symbols with specific colors; and noted the fifth animal silhouette.

You can now either travel by tram back to Crater Island, or follow the scribe to Jungle Island. If you have not previously solved the problem of the Wahrk Idol, reached the Jungle Island Fire Marble Dome, and gone on to find Gehn's Throne tower, now is your chance.

You'll probably want to go to Jungle Island, because by now you should have all the information you need to crack the Puzzle of the Twenty-Five Stones and reach the Age of the Rebel Moiety.

The Rebel Moiety Age

Finding the Rebel World
This may be one of the two or three most difficult problems in the game, but you must find your way here to successfully complete the game.

The Nature of the Moiety

At one point or another, you have to find a group of natives who call them-selves "The Moiety." Who are they? How do you go about doing this?

▶ In your explorations so far, have you seen signs of discontent in the local population? Of fear? Of rebellion?

▶ Have you noticed clues that might tell you something about the nature of Gehn's rule over the Rivenese?

▶ The Moiety is what a band of rebels on Riven call themselves. What or who might they be rebelling against?

▶ The Moiety must have a safe haven from which they can carry out their operations in the world of Riven. Is that haven likely to be on one of the islands?

▶ The Moiety must operate virtually under the nose of Gehn, the archi-tect and ruler of this world. How do they communicate with one another and with the natives whom they are trying to free?

▶ They are going to leave extremely subtle clues to teach the natives how to reach them, clues that Gehn might overlook.

Shapes, Sounds, and Symbols

Someone has gone to a lot of trouble to place subtle clues to something important throughout one particular island. These clues involve distinctive shapes, specific sounds, and certain cryptic symbols.

▶ Is there a persistent artifact that has turned up several times in your explorations? Something that appears connected to a larger mystery?

▶ There are several locations on Jungle Island where a wooden artifact is found.

▶ Each artifact is painted like an eye.

▶ Each wooden eye makes a distinctive noise when it is turned.

▶ The noise of each eye is different from the noise made by the others.

▶ Each wooden eye has a different symbol on the back. Can you deter-mine what these symbols represent?

- ▶ This can be extraordinarily subtle, but some of the eyes are associated with a shape, a different shape for each eye. Can you spot the shapes and guess what they might represent?

- ▶ Does the sound the eye makes relate in any way to the shapes?

- ▶ One wooden eye has no shape associated with it, but it makes a noise that you may have heard during your explorations. Can you identify the animal by hearing its call?

- ▶ The shapes in question are the shapes of animals.

- ▶ The wooden eyes sometimes appear in the relative positions of the actual eyes of the real animals.

- ▶ The sounds the wooden eyes make are the sounds made by those animals.

- ▶ Eventually, you should have a list of four animals, each identified by the sound it makes, each associated with a different symbol.

- ▶ Remember, you may not have the complete list.

- ▶ There is a fifth animal shape. You will need to look elsewhere to see it.

The Fifth Shape

After tracking down four of the shapes and symbols and determining what the symbols mean, you will still need one more piece to the puzzle—the fifth animal shape.

- ▶ You must search far and wide to spot this one.

- ▶ Be alert in your travels for a particular viewing perspective that seems to show an unusual or distinctive shape.

- ▶ You can identify the shape by looking for the eye. If there's something that resembles a wooden eye in the appropriate place on an object that might be an animal shape, that is one of the puzzle pieces to the Moiety World.

▶ You need to know the shape of the fifth animal. You do not need to actually reach the eye, as is the case with the others.

▶ In fact, you *can't* reach the wooden eye on this one. You can only see it from one particular vantage point.

▶ That vantage point is *not* on Jungle Island.

▶ The shape you're looking for, however, *is* on Jungle Island.

▶ There is no sound associated with this shape.

▶ You do not need to see the symbol on the back of the wooden eye associated with this shape, which is a good thing, because you can't reach it. Once you identify the shape and put it together with the information you've already acquired, the identity of the necessary symbol is more or less obvious.

Finding the Moiety Gateway

Once you have the code (a list of animals and symbols that should tell you how to use them), you must still figure out where to use it.

▶ Again, have you learned anything during your explorations that might tell you what Gehn's rule is like in Riven?

▶ Are the people happy under that rule? Are they afraid?

▶ The Moiety has been fighting against Gehn. What might his response be to their rebellion?

▶ Are there clues that might suggest how Gehn treats rebels he manages to capture?

▶ Investigate Village Lake on Jungle Island. One distinctive structure appears to be designed to eliminate rebels in a spectacular fashion.

▶ Investigating the School Room will confirm how rebels are executed.

▶ Call the device the Wahrk Gallows. Can you approach it? Can you use it to reach someplace else?

▶ Can you find the place where rebel prisoners might be held while they await their fate?

- ▶ The prisoner! He's gone!

- ▶ You were looking at the prison door when you pressed the button. Where did he go? Not out the front door.

- ▶ Okay. If a rebel group is operating on the island, couldn't they have worked out a means of rescuing those of their number who have fallen into Gehn's hands?

- ▶ Perhaps the prison cell requires a closer examination.

- ▶ Okay. *That* opens, but nothing else happens. Why? Is there anything more to be learned here? Check *everything*!

- ▶ Once you find the secret door, things will get very dark. Keep moving ahead. You'll come to some light eventually.

- ▶ Okay. Dead end. But is there anything here that might cast some light on this situation?

- ▶ Back up the tunnel. Check carefully. Is there anything you might have missed while walking in the dark?

TIP: NO, THE PROGRAM HASN'T DIED. IF YOUR SCREEN GOES COMPLETELY BLACK, IT'S JUST BECAUSE YOU'RE IN A PITCH-BLACK TUNNEL. KEEP MOVING FORWARD!

Using the Gateway

Congratulations! You've found a strange, well-hidden room with even stranger decor. The dagger symbol on the far wall is covered by water that is somehow forced to obey some very different laws of physics. Might this be the gate you've been looking for?

- ▶ Examine the room. How many stones are there? What is on the stones?

▶ Have you seen any of these shapes before?

▶ Do these shapes relate to the animal shapes you've seen already?

▶ How many shapes have you discovered?

▶ Have you learned yet what the symbols associated with each shape represent? Does this suggest how to use the shapes?

▶ Try touching the stones. Obviously, they must be touched in a particular order.

▶ *What is that order?*

▶ Do you have all of the shapes you need?

▶ There are 25 shapes in all. What number has figured prominently in Riven thus far?

▶ This is the Fifth Age, there were five sides to the Gate Room, five arms to the star symbol, five beetles on the five pillars, and five islands.

▶ You need five animal shapes entered in a particular order.

▶ You *can* solve the puzzle by brute force by trying different combinations in turn, but it will take a long time and become inordinately tedious.

▶ You can also leave this for later if you haven't acquired all of the shapes yet.

TIP: THREE OF THE SHAPES YOU ARE LOOKING FOR ARE RELATIVELY STRAIGHTFORWARD. ONE SHAPE MUST BE INFERRED BY THE SOUND MADE BY THE WOODEN EYE, BECAUSE THERE IS NO SHAPE AT THAT SITE. THE FIFTH SHAPE IS DIABOLICALLY SUBTLE AND CANNOT BE REACHED PHYSICALLY. YOU CAN SEE IT, HOWEVER, FROM ONE—AND ONLY ONE—SPOT ON ONE OF THE ISLANDS.

In the Rebel World
Okay. Now that you're in the Rebel world, what do you do now?

▶ Explore your surroundings. Where are you?

▶ At some point in your explorations, a young woman enters your room. You can't understand her language, but she certainly seems to want to communicate *something* important.

▶ Listen closely to her speech. Did you hear a name you recognized?

▶ What does she give you?

▶ What does she seem to want you to do?

▶ You're obviously not going anywhere for a while. Maybe you should do what she says.

▶ After a time, the woman returns with something else. What does it look like?

▶ What do you see in the image in the book?

▶ Could this be the way back?

 **TIP:** WHAT THE WOMAN GIVES YOU IS CRUCIAL TO THE SUCCESSFUL COMPLETION OF THE GAME.

Once you have the journal and the Trap Book in your possession, you're ready to return to Jungle Island via the linking book the woman lays open on the table.

Gehn's World

Reaching Gehn's World
Finding out how to reach Gehn's world is probably the single most difficult problem to solve. The clues are subtle, the components of the puzzle obscure and widely scattered. Good luck!

The Linking Books

▶ Travel between different Ages—the various created worlds—is accomplished through special books.

▶ Have you seen any books yet during your travels, other than the journals or the Trap Book, that is?

▶ Such books would be very well protected.

▶ Such books require a great deal of power to activate them.

▶ Such books could be expected to be located in convenient places all over Riven, where Gehn could reach them quickly if necessary. But they must also be in a place that would keep out the natives.

▶ After opening each of the Fire Marble Domes so far, could you see anything through the small glass window?

▶ Something like a book?

▶ The Fire Marble Domes are repositories for books that link to Gehn's private hideaway.

TIP: YOU ONLY NEED TO OPEN ONE OF THE FIRE MARBLE DOMES TO ACCESS A LINKING BOOK. THE ONLY REASON TO TRY OPENING ALL OF THE FIRE MARBLE DOMES IS SO THAT YOU CAN IDENTIFY THE CODE SYMBOL OF EACH ONE. YOU CAN LATER CORRELATE THAT CODE SYMBOL WITH A PARTICULAR COLOR, LEARNED DURING YOUR INVESTIGATIONS OF THE COLOR WHEEL IN GEHN'S VIEWING CHAMBER BENEATH PLATEAU ISLAND.

Opening the Fire Marble Dome Locks

Opening a Fire Marble Dome with its kinetoscope isn't enough. When you stop the rotation and open the outer dome, you are still faced with a lock—five vertical sliders that must be moved along a horizontal scale to specific positions. Learning what those positions are is one of the major puzzles of the game.

- ▶ The horizontal scale looks like a ruler, laid out in five groups of five.

- ▶ The domes were built by Gehn. Where might he have left a note for himself, a reminder of the combination?

- ▶ By now, you should have learned the first 10 numerals of the Rivenese numbering system.

- ▶ By now, too, you should have seen Gehn's lab journal, and searched through it carefully.

- ▶ Is there anything in Gehn's lab journal that looks like a string of several numbers?

- ▶ Might that be the code?

- ▶ The slider scale enables you to enter numbers as high as 25. Unfortunately, you only know the first 10 numbers.

- ▶ Some of the numbers in Gehn's journal may be higher than 10.

- ▶ Can you take what you know of the Rivenese numbering system and extrapolate what the rest of the numbers look like? Enough, at least, for you to take a guess at what the numbers in the journal are?

TIP: RIVENESE NUMERALS—DERIVED FROM THE COUNTING SYSTEM OF LOST D'NI—ARE BASE FIVE. INSTEAD OF COUNTING BY TENS, A RIVENESE WOULD COUNT BY FIVES. "FIVE" IS WRITTEN AS A ONE ROTATED 90 DEGREES COUNTERCLOCKWISE; "TEN" IS A ROTATED TWO, "FIFTEEN" IS A ROTATED THREE, AND "TWENTY" IS A ROTATED FOUR. OTHER NUMERALS ARE CREATED BY COMBINING SYMBOLS. "EIGHT" IS A COMBINATION OF THE SYMBOLS FOR FIVE AND THREE. "SIXTEEN" IS FIFTEEN AND ONE. THE ONLY WILDCARD IN THE SERIES IS "25," WHICH LOOKS LIKE AN "X" IN A BOX. FORTUNATELY, YOU WON'T HAVE TO FIGURE OUT NUMBERS HIGHER THAN 25!

Once you think you have the sequence, move each slider to the appropriate position on the scale and press the button. If you've worked out the numbers correctly, the inner portion of the dome will open, giving you access to the linking book.

Unfortunately, you're *still* not home free. The book is open, but it needs power—lots of power—to work. Power to all of the Fire Marble Dome linking books in Riven comes from one place, and you need to solve a final puzzle to figure out how to turn on the power.

Finding the Fire Marble Puzzle

There is one trek you yet must make in order to power up all of the Fire Marble Domes on Riven.

▶ What facility have you seen thus far in your travels that might conceivably provide a great deal of power to the Fire Marble Domes on all of the Riven islands?

▶ Is there a part of that facility you have not yet explored?

▶ You will need to raise a drawbridge from inside the facility. If you did this when you reached the Golden Dome from Crater Island earlier, then the path is open to the upper level of the dome from the Gate Room on Temple Island.

TIP: YOU WON'T BE PREPARED TO SOLVE THIS FINAL PUZZLE UNLESS YOU KNOW (OR CAN GUESS) WHAT COLORS ARE ASSOCIATED WITH THE DIFFERENT FIRE MARBLE DOMES, AND KNOW (OR CAN GUESS USING THE 3-D TOPOLOGICAL RELIEF MAPS YOU SAW ON PLATEAU ISLAND), WHERE ON EACH ISLAND EACH FIRE MARBLE DOME IS. SOME GUESSWORK IS UNAVOIDABLE, UNFORTUNATELY. ONE COLOR IS MISSING AND YOU HAVE NOT YET VISITED ONE ISLAND, SO YOU DON'T KNOW PRECISELY WHERE THE FIFTH FIRE MARBLE DOME IS LOCATED.

Solving the Fire Marble Puzzle

After finding the Fire Marble Puzzle in the upper level of the Golden Dome (accessed by way of the elevated bridge from Position 3 in the Gate Room), you can try to solve it. The puzzle consists of arrays of 25 holes in each of 25 larger squares.

▶ You've seen this pattern of squares before.

▶ At one time, this world was a single large island. Because Gehn's worlds don't last, at some point in the past the original continent was "riven" into five unequal pieces.

▶ Can you picture the graphical outlines of each island on the large array?

▶ Can you further plot the locations of the Fire Marble Domes on the different island shapes?

▶ You should have worked out the geography of each dome back on Plateau Island.

▶ You may need to return to Plateau Island and study the maps in the Map Room again, paying particular attention to where each Fire Marble Dome is located.

▶ The puzzle provides you with six colored marbles.

▶ You only need five. There's one extra. Which might it be?

▶ Try placing each of five colored marbles in the appropriate holes. When you think you have it right, go back down the passageway to the switch on the wall. Press the switch and something resembling an enormous press will come down and cover the marble array. When a white button appears under the switch, click it.

TIP: IF YOU HAVE THE RIGHT COLORED MARBLES IN THE CORRECT PLACES, A HUGE EXPLOSION (A RUSH OF AIR AND POWER) WILL FILL THE PASSAGEWAY, TUGGING AT DANGLING CABLES AND OTHER LOOSE PARTS. IF YOU HAVE IT WRONG, NOTHING WILL HAPPEN. TRY GOING BACK TO THE MARBLE ARRAY AND SETTING UP ANOTHER PATTERN.

When you have the right combination and hear and see that rush of wind, you have successfully provided power to all of the linking books. You can go to any Fire Marble Dome now, access its linking book, and travel to Gehn's hideaway age.

Gehn's World

When you open one of the linking books inside a Fire Marble Dome, you will get a glimpse of another world… a strange, red-lit world of pyramidal growths, with a structure of some kind atop one of the largest. This is a different Age or world created by Gehn as the location of his private dwelling.

Touch the image and you are transported to Gehn's home, and for the second time in your quest, you find yourself behind bars.

Other linking books are visible around the cage, each identified by its own island graphic. None of them is powered, however. A plate with a star symbol is on the bars of your cage. When you press the button in the center of the plate, Gehn appears for a little chat.

▶ He seems friendly enough. He's eager to impress you with the fact that you have probably heard incorrect information about him.

▶ If you have not reacquired the Trap Book from the Moiety, he will ask you to find it for him—not realizing its true nature.

▶ If you *have* reacquired the Trap Book (which he thinks is a linking book back to D'ni), he will consider using it but asks you to go through first.

▶ If you trap Gehn before he powers up the Linking Books, you'll have to find the power switch yourself.

▶ If you do not touch the book, he will give you time to think about it. He will also turn on the power to the Linking Books around your cage, enabling you free access to any part of Riven. He does ask you, however, to refrain from visiting Catherine, whom he's been forced to separate from the rebels for her safety as well as his.

▶ Can you deduce which symbol represents Catherine's Prison Island?

▶ Whom do you trust now? Atrus, who sent you on this quest in the first place? Catherine, the leader of the Rebel Moiety, a woman you've never met? Or Gehn, who admits to having tried to kill his son once, but who now is trying to make amends and who needs your help to save Riven and its people?

 **TIP:** BY NOW, THROUGH YOUR EXPLORATIONS AND BY READING THE JOURNALS OF ATRUS, CATHERINE, AND GEHN, YOU SHOULD HAVE FORMED AN IDEA ABOUT WHO IS TELLING THE TRUTH, WHO TO BELIEVE, AND WHO TO HELP.

Prison Island

The fifth island of Riven is a tiny speck lost in a vast expanse of sea, so far from the other four islands that you cannot even see it on the horizon. Most of the island is embraced by the stump of a titanic tree, with roots cradling naked rock and extending into the sea. A building—Catherine's prison—rises from the stump.

You can only reach the island from Gehn's universe by accessing the Prison Island's Linking Book. You will materialize at the island's Fire Marble Dome, which is built alongside the main island and connected to it by a short walkway. Inside, you are faced with a puzzle: Three keys, each of which makes a distinct sound and a lever to operate the lock when the correct code is entered. There is also an elevator control to the right and above. You do not yet have the information you need to operate the locking mechanism, but you can take the elevator up to Catherine's holding cell and talk to her.

▶ What's your initial reaction? Do you trust her?

▶ What does she want you to do?

▶ She fears that Gehn is using you, *watching* you. Remember the peeping-Tom image in Gehn's viewing chamber?

▶ If you don't have it yet, you will need to get the Trap Book and Catherine's journal from the Moiety.

▶ If you've already visited the Moiety, you already have everything you need to capture Gehn.

TIP: YOU MUST FACE GEHN AGAIN AND GET HIM TO USE THE TRAP BOOK IN ORDER TO RESCUE CATHERINE AND WIN THE GAME.

IT IS ALSO POSSIBLE TO TRAP GEHN *BEFORE* VISITING CATHERINE. IF YOU CAN FIND THE CODE TO HER CELL BEFORE VISITING PRISON ISLAND, YOU CAN RESCUE HER IMMEDIATELY.

End Game

Use the Fire Marble Dome outside Catherine's prison to return to Gehn's home. You can summon him again by clicking on the button that has reset itself on the bars to your cage. You now have two goals: get Gehn to use the Trap Book, and learn the combination to the lock on Catherine's prison.

The Trap Book

Gehn must touch the image on the Trap Book for it to imprison him.

▶ How does the Trap Book work?

▶ If you've played the game Myst, you've used Trap Books before. Atrus's sons, Sirrus and Achenar, you may recall, had been trapped inside Trap Books and were trying to escape.

▶ If someone is already caught inside a Trap Book, he or she will exchange places with the *next* person to touch the Trap Book's picture.

▶ Does this suggest a way to convince Gehn to touch the image?

The Code to the Prison

After exchanging places with Gehn, you are outside the bars and have access to his quarters. A lever on one window ledge lowers the bars of your cage, giving you access to all five books.

▶ You will have to search for the code.

▶ It is likely to be well hidden.

▶ The code wasn't in his journal in the lab. If the secret is anywhere, it must be here.

▶ Search his home carefully. (He certainly won't be coming back to interrupt you!)

▶ The ladder rungs on the wall lead to his bedroom downstairs.

▶ His bedroom contains lots of odds and ends pertaining to his private life.

▶ You are searching for something that gives you a clue to the series of sounds that will open the lock to Catherine's prison.

TIP: CHECK GEHN'S PERSONAL BELONGINGS CAREFULLY. HE WOULDN'T LEAVE INFORMATION LIKE THIS IN A JOURNAL. THE CLUE WILL BE HIDDEN WHERE HE CAN EASILY ACCESS IT.

IF YOU TRAP GEHN *BEFORE* HE TURNS ON THE POWER TO THE LINKING BOOKS, YOU'LL HAVE TO FIND THE LEVER THAT TURNS ON THE POWER YOURSELF.

Once you have the code, you can return to Catherine's prison and free her. She tells you that Riven is doomed, that the only hope now is to signal Atrus by using the telescope to crack open the Star Fissure, sealed over now by metal plates. While you do that, she will arrange to get the Rivenese natives to safety in the Moiety's Age.

By the time you reach the Prison Island's Fire Marble Dome, it is closed and turning again, evidence that Catherine has used it to escape first to Gehn's world, and then to one of the islands of Riven. You must go through and, somehow, use the telescope to open the Star Fissure.

The Telescope

Yes! The strange device you first encountered on *Riven was* a telescope, of sorts, and now its operation is the key to your escape.

WARNING! DON'T TRY TO OPERATE THIS DEVICE UNTIL THE VERY END OF THE GAME—OR YOU'RE IN REAL TROUBLE!

▶ Do the controls work? Have you turned on the power?

▶ If not, you'd better do so. Where might the power be coming from?

▶ Is the pipe leading to the device on the right side of the apparatus a clue? Where does the pipe come from?

▶ Have you opened the hatch cover on the ground?

▶ Have you learned where the combination might be recorded?

▶ Who might have that combination?

▶ When you rescue Catherine from Prison Island, she tells you where the combination is and what you must do.

▶ Okay, you've got power and the controls work. You're trying to lower the telescope to break the glass and open the Star Fissure. Something seems to be blocking the telescope as it slides down the mounting rails.

▶ Check the supports carefully.

▶ There's a clue in Catherine's journal.

▶ What you're trying to do is *not* normally a good idea—breaking the glass and opening the fissure. Isn't it likely that some sort of safety feature might have been built into this thing?

▶ Look for a pin blocking the telescope's movement and move it out of the way.

TIP: REMEMBER LAB CLASS AT THE MICROSCOPE IN SCHOOL, TURNING THE FOCUS AND ACCIDENTALLY DRIVING THE OBJECTIVE LENS DOWN THROUGH THE GLASS SLIDE? THIS IS WHAT YOU ARE ATTEMPTING TO DO HERE. YOU MUST OPEN THE WINDOW—BUT TAKE A MOMENT TO LOOK AT THE STARS MYSTERIOUSLY EVIDENT THROUGH THE PORT, FOCUSING ON THEM THROUGH THE EYEPIECE—AND THEN USE THE LEVER TO THE RIGHT TO DRIVE THE TIP OF THE DEVICE DOWN THROUGH THE GLASS.

You've done it! This cracks the glass, and then the steel plating, the entire telescope and its supporting structure topple into the whirlwind fury of the open fissure. Riven is dying, crumbling around you as the sky grows black and the ground trembles. Atrus, summoned from D'ni, appears and, a moment later, Catherine joins him. The natives are safe, and the universes need not fear Gehn's further misguided meddling…

…*if*, of course, you succeeded in both trapping Gehn and freeing Catherine. The ending will be quite different if you've failed somewhere along the line.

That, of course, is why you bought this guide! Go back and try Riven again. Enjoy the complex beauty of this alien world.

And this time see if you can open the gateway to a *better* world.

CHAPTER FOUR
The Islands of Riven:
Maps and Specifics

This is a SUNNER chapter. It contains both hints and tips for playing the game, and specific hints for solving certain key puzzles. Reading this chapter before playing Riven will rob the game of some of its fun and suspense.

Like Chapter 3, this chapter is divided into sections that describe each area within Riven. This time, however, each area is mapped out in detail. You can use these maps to determine where you are, where you've been, and where you want to go, but you'll definitely lose some of the mystery and suspense along the way.

Also included in this chapter are lists of the puzzles and problems that must be solved *in order* for you to proceed through the game, along with some specific hints and tips for solving them. It stops short of giving away the entire solution to each problem, but it definitely gives away an awful lot!

Temple Island

You start your adventure on Temple Island, south of the Star Fissure and the Telescope. You must untangle the mysteries of the Gate Room, the Great Golden Dome, and the Temple.

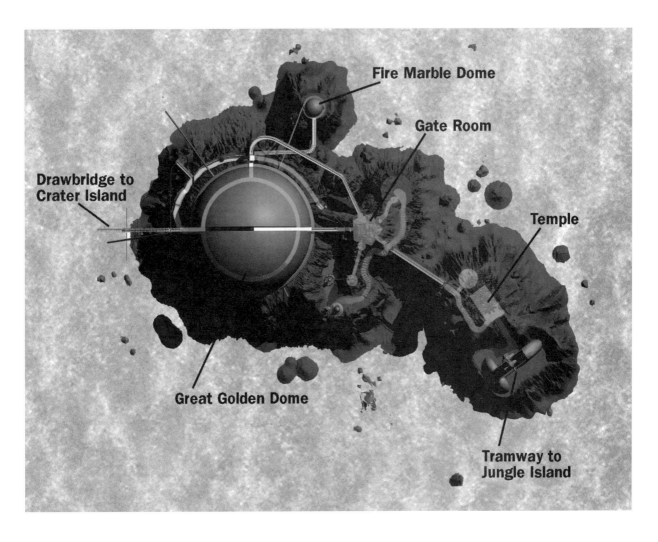

Fire Marble Dome

Gate Room

Drawbridge to Crater Island

Temple

Great Golden Dome

Tramway to Jungle Island

Puzzles and Problems on Temple Island

▶ Solve the puzzle of the Gate Room. How do you get where you need to go and open the gates and grates you need to open?

▶ Provide power to the telescope.

▶ How do you reach the Golden Dome?

▶ What can you turn on in the Golden Dome?

▶ The Fire Marble Dome Puzzle. How do you open it? What symbol is associated with it?

▶ The Temple. What can you learn about its designer? How do you open the outer Temple door?

After completing your initial explorations of Temple Island, you should have:

▶ Figured out how to use the Gate Room to access any of the five doors.

▶ Lowered the grates that block two of the doors.

▶ Turned on the power to the telescope.

▶ Explored the Golden Dome and switched on power to the West Drawbridge to Crater Island and the drawbridge between the Gate Room and the Dome.

▶ Opened the main door of the Temple and found the tram to Jungle Island.

▶ You will not be able to open the Fire Marble Dome on your first visit. You must do this on a return visit.

Puzzles and Problems on Jungle Island

Ride the mag-lev tram from Temple Island to Jungle Island. This area is larger and has a lot more in the way of secrets and mysteries than did Temple Island.

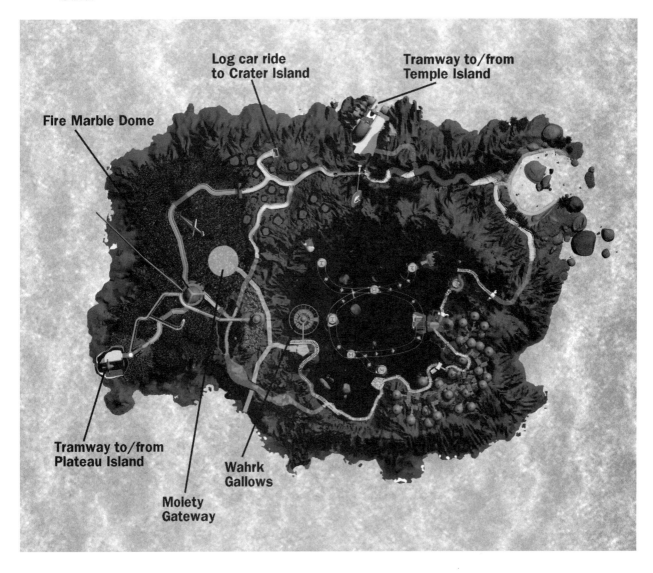

Log car ride
to Crater Island

Tramway to/from
Temple Island

Fire Marble Dome

Tramway to/from
Plateau Island

Wahrk
Gallows

Moiety
Gateway

▶ What is the purpose of the wooden eyes?

▶ Can you link each eye with a particular animal, through a particular sound the animal makes and/or through the silhouette of that animal?

▶ Can you find *four* wooden eyes?

▶ Can you find a place where you can learn the meaning of the symbols on the back of each wooden eye?

▶ Figure out how to lower the submarine. Then learn how to operate it to travel around Village Lake.

▶ *The Control Room*: Can you find a way to lower three of the five ladders to gain access to key landings around the inside of Village Lake?

▶ *The School Room*: Can you learn what you need to know about D'ni numbers?

▶ *The Wahrk Gallows*: You must close the central opening on the Wahrk Gallows before you can explore all of its secrets.

▶ What is the secret of the Wahrk Idol in the jungle? Can you find a way to reach the catwalks you can see among the trees or the Fire Marble Dome you see turning above you?

▶ There is actually more than one way to reach the Fire Marble Dome. When you do reach it, can you stop the turning and learn the symbol associated with it?

▶ After penetrating the Wahrk Idol's secret, can you find Gehn's raised throne? What can you do there that you must do to continue your explorations?

▶ *Back to the Wahrk Gallows*: After closing the central opening, can you find the prison holding cell and the secret beyond it? Do you have all of the information you need to solve the Puzzle of the Twenty-five Stones?

▶ Can you find the log-car ride that carries you from Jungle Island to Crater Island? (This one's easy—almost as easy as falling off a log!)

After you've explored Jungle Island, you should have:

▶ Collected four symbols from four wooden eyes and determined what the symbols mean. This is necessary to solve the puzzle of the gateway to the Moiety Age.

▶ Used the submarine to complete a circuit of the lake. You may not have been able to access the Wahrk Gallows the first time around, but you should have reached the Control Tower to lower the ladders, and entered the school room to discover what there is to be learned there.

▶ Found the Wahrk Idol. You may have learned its secret the first time around, or you may need to come back to Jungle Island later from an unexpected direction.

▶ Now, or later, you will need to reach the Jungle Island Fire Marble Dome, learn the appropriate symbol, and visit Gehn's throne. You must reach Gehn's throne to gain access to the Wahrk Gallows.

▶ Once you have access to the Wahrk Gallows, you can find Gehn's prison, solve the problem of finding the gateway to the Moiety Age, and at least begin thinking about how to solve *that* devious puzzle.

Puzzles and Problems on Crater Island

You ride the log car to another island, this one known as Crater Island. You arrive rather unceremoniously, dumped down a chute and dropped into a chipper that, fortunately for you, is unpowered at the moment.

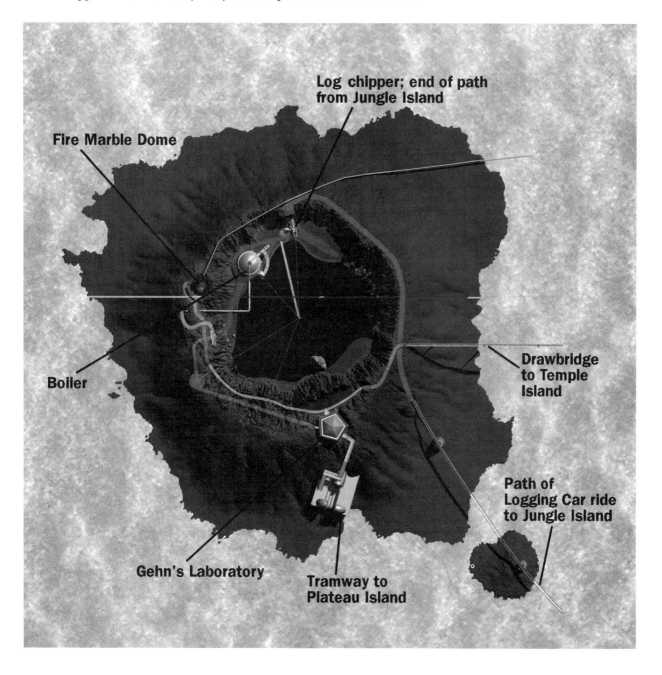

Log chipper; end of path from Jungle Island

Fire Marble Dome

Boiler

Drawbridge to Temple Island

Path of Logging Car ride to Jungle Island

Gehn's Laboratory

Tramway to Plateau Island

▶ Can you solve the puzzle of the boiler? To reach the ladder and passageway in the center of the room beyond the door, you must raise the floor grating, ensuring that the tank is drained of water and that the furnace is off. How do you go about doing this?

▶ After raising the grating and crossing the drainage pipe in the middle of the boiler tank, you can take a long, dark crawl and climb that will deposit you high atop the mountains surrounding the lake. Can you find a path leading over the crest of the ridge and down to a railed balcony?

▶ The apparatus at the end of the long catwalk leading into the mountain is for catching frogs. Can you catch one using the trap and the bait?

▶ The large building visible on the side of the cliff is Gehn's book-making laboratory. The only door you can reach is locked. Getting in is a problem; it requires an approach from an unexpected direction.

▶ The double doors above the railed balcony on the cliff lead to the frog-catching apparatus, but there's more to this site than meets the eye. Can you find the Fire Marble Dome for Crater Island, and can you find the hidden kinetoscope that stops it?

TIP: THERE'S QUITE A LOT OF INTEREST IN GEHN'S LAB, WHERE HE HAS OBVIOUSLY BEEN EXPERIMENTING WITH HOW TO MAKE PAPER AND BIND BOOKS. YOU MIGHT ALSO GUESS WHY HE'S BEEN CATCHING FROGS: HE TAKES AN EXTRACT FROM THEM AND SMOKES IT IN HIS PIPE. YES, OUR FRIEND GEHN SMOKES FROG EXTRACT, SLAUGHTERING HUNDREDS OF THE TINY, BEAUTIFUL CREATURES TO FEED HIS HABIT. HIS JOURNAL DISCUSSES HIS SEARCH FOR A BETTER, SMOOTHER FROG EXTRACT. WHAT DOES THIS TELL YOU ABOUT THE MAN?

After penetrating Gehn's laboratory, you'll gain access to an important source of additional clues that you'll need in your quest. Also, the path is open that leads back to the Golden Dome via the bridge, or you can return to Jungle Island on the log cart, or you can summon a tram from the front of Gehn's lab.

After completing your explorations of Crater Island, you should have:

▶ Solved the puzzles of the boiler, the central power valve, and the ventilation fan duct.

▶ Discovered the location of this island's Fire Marble Dome.

▶ Found and read Gehn's lab journal.

▶ Found in Gehn's lab journal a series of D'ni numbers.

▶ Found the catwalk and bridge leading back to the Great Golden Dome on Temple Island.

▶ Found the tram outside Gehn's lab.

▶ Learned quite a lot about Gehn and his personal habits.

The tram takes you to the next unexplored island, Plateau Island.

Puzzles and Problems on Plateau Island

The tram from Gehn's lab deposits you on Plateau Island. Note that, while you can get out on the left side of the tram, there is a door visible to the right. Take the left-hand side for now, but keep thinking about how you can gain across to the other side of the tram line.

Plateau Island contains some of the grandest and most spectacular scenery yet seen in the world of Riven. It also holds the key to the most fiendish of Riven's puzzles.

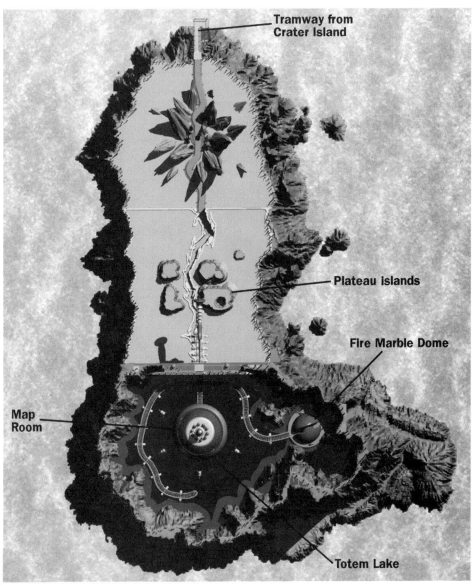

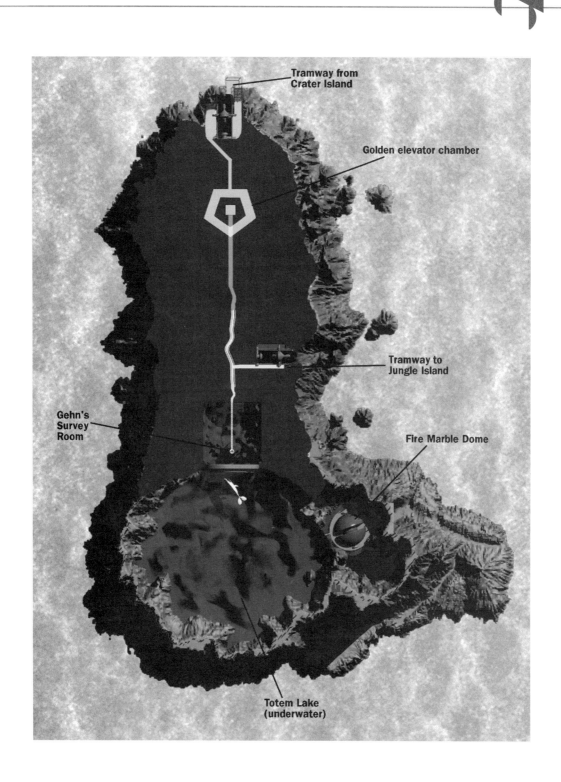

Tramway from
Crater Island

Golden elevator chamber

Tramway to
Jungle Island

Gehn's
Survey
Room

Fire Marble Dome

Totem Lake
(underwater)

- ▶ The overhead view of the plateau islands and the corresponding 3-D relief views of each sector of each island in the Map Room together constitute both problem and puzzle. What are you supposed to do with the information displayed here?

- ▶ This island's Fire Marble Dome is visible beyond a cleft in the rock wall just past the lake on which the Map Room rests. The kinetoscope, when you find it, is broken. Can you open the dome anyway?

- ▶ Can you figure out how to reach the other side of the tram?

- ▶ *The Viewing Chamber Puzzles.* When you reach the other side, you will encounter one of Gehn's scribes, and, if you pursue him, you will watch him vanish into another tram car—but *not* the one you arrived in. The passageway beyond the tram car station, however, leads to an underwater viewing chamber that offers several important clues to several of Riven's other puzzles. Can you find them?

When you've finished with Plateau Island, you should:

- ▶ Have a good guess as to the identity of the fifth animal shape, which will let you solve the Moiety Puzzle on Jungle Island.

- ▶ Have noted the Fire Marble symbols and matched most of them with a different color. This will help you solve the Gehn's Age Puzzle.

- ▶ Have learned which patterns of squares represent which islands.

- ▶ Have solved the Map Puzzle and identified which sector on each island holds a Fire Marble Dome. This, too, is necessary for the solution to the puzzle of Gehn's Age.

- ▶ Taken the newly discovered tram back to Jungle Island and learned the Wahrk Idol's secret, if you didn't find it earlier.

Puzzles and Problems of Reaching the Moiety Age

You reach the Moiety Age from Jungle Island. When you arrive, a woman named Nelah gives you Catherine's journal and the Trap Book that was taken from you at the beginning of your quest.

Collecting all of the clues you need, however, is a bit of a chore.

▶ Can you solve the problem of finding the gateway to the Moiety Age? You need to learn how to use the submarine to reach the Wahrk Gallows. You also need to have found Gehn's Throne and learned how to close the base of the gallows. Then you must find your way up the gallows to the prison cell, learn the cell's secret, find your way through the darkness, learn how to light your way back, and finally (!) discover the doorway to the gateway.

▶ After finding the gateway, you must know the code for opening it. You must have found and examined four wooden eyes at various points in Jungle Island, and associated each with a particular animal silhouette or, in one case, with the call of an animal that you have seen on the island. You must have associated each animal with a symbol which, at the school room, you've discovered is a number.

▶ With four animals and four numbers, you're almost there, but you also need to discover what the *fifth* animal silhouette is—the one in the underwater viewing chamber on Plateau Island. You will not be able to reach the wooden eye associated with this silhouette, but you will be able to infer which number is associated with it. You may have seen a duplicate of this eye in Gehn's lab.

▶ Finally, you must touch the proper stones in the gateway room in the proper order. The order is obvious, based on the number associated with each silhouette. If you get the order or the animal graphic wrong, nothing will happen and you must reset the stones by touching each in reverse order or by pressing a sixth stone. When you have the stones in the correct order, the water that covers the far wall will flow away through side channels, the dagger panel will open, enabling you to reach a linking book that will take you to the Moiety Age.

You will be knocked unconscious by a rebel blowgun dart, awakening in a small chamber. At this point, all you need to do is guess what the woman is telling you to do, and do it.

After finishing the Rebel Age, you should have:

▶ The Trap Book taken from you at the beginning of the quest.

▶ Catherine's journal, which contains information you will need later.

The woman will return with another linking book. Touch the image on the book, and you will be returned to the Room of the Twenty-five Stones on Jungle Island.

Puzzles and Problems of Reaching Gehn's Age

Reaching the alternate reality where Gehn lives when he is not playing god and lording it over the inhabitants of Riven involves some of the toughest puzzles in the game.

▶ Can you learn the first part of the secret of the Fire Marble Domes and open the outer shell?

▶ Can you acquire the five-digit code that opens the inner lock and gives you access to a linking book?

▶ Have you learned how to read the D'ni symbols for the numerals 1 through 10? Having done that, can you figure out the pattern the numbers use in order to figure out the numerals 11 through 24? Finally, there is a chance that one symbol will represent the numeral 25. If that numeral occurs in the sequence, can you guess what it is?

▶ Have you associated a particular graphic symbol with each of the four domes?

▶ Have you learned what colors are represented by those symbols? Three of them are easy, but a fourth must be arrived at by guesswork.

▶ Have you reached the Map Room on Plateau Island, learned its secrets, and plotted the locations of five Fire Marble Domes on Riven?

▶ Have you deduced that the linking books in the Fire Marble Domes require power, figured out where that power must come from, and learned how to reach a final puzzle that will turn on that power?

▶ Have you solved the Marble Puzzle, which turns on the power to the linking books? You must correctly place five out of six colored marbles on a grid of 625 holes. You will only know three of the colors for certain; the fourth and fifth require a guesswork choice among the three remaining marbles.

If the correct marbles are in the proper holes when you pull the lever on the wall and then press a white button, an explosion of air around the marble device will tell you that the linking books are now powered and ready to use.

Once you reach Gehn's Age, what happens next depends on whether or not you have reached the Moiety Age and reacquired the Trap Book. You will have the opportunity to come and go among the five different islands of Riven. In addition, if you have not yet done so, you must solve the problem of reaching the Rebel Age to reacquire your stolen Trap Book. You may also visit Catherine on Prison Island, but each time you do so you will return to Gehn's Age until either you successfully trap him or he kills you.

After finishing Gehn's Age, you should have:

▶ Solved the Marble Puzzle that gives you access to Gehn's Age through any of the Fire Marble Domes.

▶ Found yourself in a prison cell in Gehn's home.

▶ Seen the five linking books arrayed about your prison cell, and recognized each as a link—initially unpowered—to one of the five islands of Riven.

▶ Found a button that calls Gehn into the room for a little chat.

- ▶ Listened to Gehn and either watched him turn on the power for all of the linking books or trapped him, escaped from the cage, and turned on the power for yourself.

- ▶ Used the Trap Book to capture Gehn and escape from your cell. This might be accomplished on a subsequent trip, rather than during the first visit to this Age.

- ▶ Used the linking book to the fifth island to visit Catherine, and seen the coded lock on her cell. This might be accomplished on this visit or on a later one.

- ▶ Found the key (a series of specific sounds) somewhere in Gehn's residence that enables you to open Catherine's cell.

- ▶ Returned to Catherine's island and freed her.

Don't give up now! You're almost there!

WARNING! WHEN YOU SUMMON GEHN, HE TAKES THE TRAP BOOK FROM YOU AND THEN OFFERS YOU THE OPPORTUNITY OF GOING THROUGH AHEAD OF HIM. YOU MAY REFUSE. HE WILL ONLY GIVE YOU THREE CHANCES, HOWEVER, BEFORE HE DECIDES THAT YOU ARE NOT WORTH THE EFFORT, AND THEN HE KILLS YOU.

Puzzles and Problems on Catherine's Island

Although Gehn asks you not to, there is nothing stopping you from using the linking book outside your cell in his residence. Use it to journey to Prison Island where Catherine is being held prisoner. You can talk to Catherine, but you will not be able to free her from her prison cell unless you can crack the code to the three-keyed lock you encounter in the elevator.

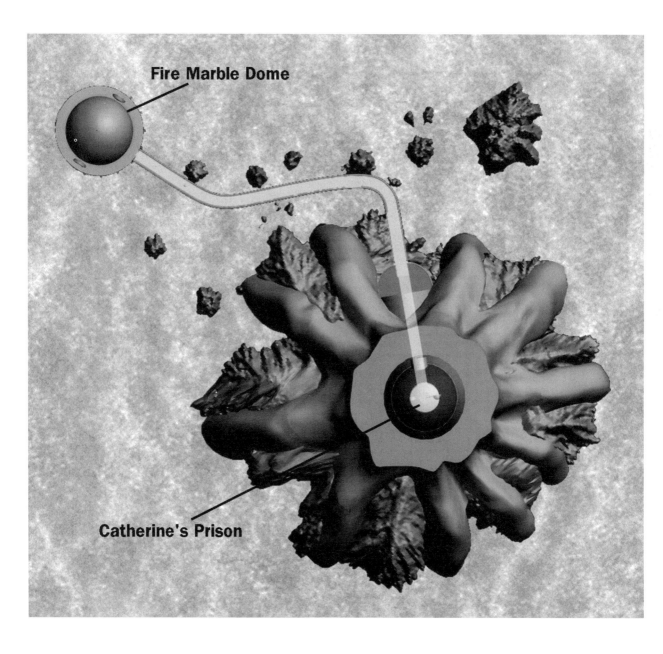

Fire Marble Dome

Catherine's Prison

▶ Can you find the code to the lock somewhere in Gehn's residence? You can only do this if you've successfully trapped him in Atrus's Trap Book.

▶ Can you find the lever that opens your former cell? You need to open the cage in order to regain access to the five linking books.

When you leave Catherine's island for the last time, you should have:

▶ Freed Catherine from her cell.

▶ Received instructions from her regarding the telescope and the Star Fissure. You will need to solve one final puzzle before you successfully complete the game.

The Telescope Puzzle

You have one last puzzle to face now and, ironically, it's within a handful of steps from the very spot at which you first arrived on Riven. The telescope is the device that looks something like a steel ice-cream cone suspended above a round hatch set into some iron plates on the ground. An eyepiece gives you a view of the hatch… or what's beyond it, presumably, if the hatch is open. A button raises or lowers the telescope for focus; a lever determines which way—up or down—the device moves.

Your goal is to open the hatch, and reveal a glass window looking into a field of stars within a deep fissure in the ground. Then use the tip of the telescope to break the glass and end the Riven Age.

▶ Have you figured out how to turn on the power to the telescope?

▶ Have you learned where the code to the hatch's locking device is kept, and used it to open the hatch?

▶ Have you found the locking pin that protects the glass from the telescope's descent?

▶ Have you smashed the glass?

 **WARNING!** DON'T OPERATE THE TELESCOPE UNTIL YOU'RE SURE YOU'RE READY TO END THE GAME! ONCE THE GLASS IS BROKEN, THERE'S NO TURNING BACK!

You have completed your final task when you have:

▶ Powered up the telescope.

▶ Unlocked the safety pin.

▶ Used the telescope to break the glass.

A few moments after Riven's final Armageddon has commenced, Atrus appears. What occurs next, and what he says, will depend on whether or not you have successfully done everything required of you, or whether some tasks remain unfinished when you finally open the Star Fissure.

You will have won the most complete victory possible if, when you open the Star Fissure, you have:

▶ Trapped Gehn.

▶ Freed Catherine.

If either or both of these tasks remain unfinished, you will be treated to a different ending, one less joyful than that resulting from complete success.

CHAPTER FIVE
Walking Through the Fifth Age

This is a SUNNER chapter. Reading this chapter *before* playing the game will rob you of quite a bit of the mystery and surprise associated with the saga of *Riven*.

This chapter takes you virtually step by step through the entire game, telling the story from the point of view of an adventurer like yourself. Remember, though, that *Riven* is a remarkably open-ended game. There is no one "right path" to take, and no specific order in which the puzzles must be found and solved. Your path through *Riven* will almost certainly be quite different from the one outlined here.

Things were not working out as Atrus had planned.

After I rescued him from his prison in D'ni, I spent considerable time exploring the worlds of Myst at my leisure. Although my excursions were most enjoyable, I confess I was relieved when he contacted me and asked me to perform another task for him. The lack of purpose to my wanderings had begun to pall, and I looked forward to a new adventure.

But Gehn seems to have the upper hand from the start.

I'm afraid Atrus was right to be so worried! If I'm reading this correctly, the new crisis is more worse than the one precipitated by his sons. Gehn—Atrus's father—is that "greater foe" he spoke of when I rescued him in the Myst affair, a man who cannot be allowed to continue his predations on the world of Riven. Atrus handed me a trap book (I remembered those from the Isle of Myst!) and told me I must use it to capture Gehn. He also gave me his personal journal, in the hopes that I might find clues there that would assist in my quest.

I placed my hand on the Linking Book and was transported to Riven, finding myself in a small chamber, looking out onto stark cliffs with a view of the sea beyond. I was struck by the sight of a strange mechanical contrivance in the space between the cliffs but had no time to investigate before bars arose in front of me, leaving me a prisoner! I didn't know whether Gehn somehow had known I was coming or whether any stranger coming to this Age would have been thusly imprisoned. It didn't matter. My mission was already at risk, and I had scarcely begun.

I was turning my options over in my mind—not that I had many—when someone casually strolled into my limited field of view. His dress had a military look to it, although he appeared somewhat uncomfortable, even unnatural, as though the uniform were wearing him. He carried a sheathed knife or short sword on his belt, and I surmised that he was some sort of militiaman or guard recruited from among the inhabitants of Riven. He seemed quite surprised to see me, but after recovering from his shock, he moved closer, jabbering incomprehensibly. Wondering what to make of this anomaly, I was caught unprepared when he reached between the bars of my cage and wrested the Trap Book from my grasp. His satisfaction was short-lived, however; he had scarcely opened the book when he slapped at his neck as though stung, and then collapsed on the ground, the book falling from his fingers. Whether he was dead or merely unconscious, I could not tell.

After a few stunned seconds, I observed the body being dragged away by an agency unseen. A masked figure then appeared, dressed all in black with a red sash and headband, and sporting on his belt a long tube, presumably a blow gun for poison darts. He stooped and retrieved the Trap Book, threw a lever on the ground that began to lower the bars of my prison, smashing the mechanism with his weapon, and then hurried off. As soon as the bars were down and I was free to move about, neither the guard nor my mysterious benefactor was anywhere to be seen.

My situation was only marginally improved. True, I was no longer behind bars, but I was bereft of the Trap Book, the one tool I had brought with me on this quest.

At least I still had the journal Atrus had given me! Perhaps perusing it would yield clues that would enable me to complete my mission, despite the loss of the Trap Book. I decided that after reading it carefully, I would extend the journal with notes of my own discoveries. At this juncture I had only that journal and my own wits to depend upon.

It appears that much now depends on the success of my efforts: the rescue of Catherine and the relocation of the inhabitants of Riven before this Age's inevitable collapse, not to mention my own eventual return home. All are contingent upon my capturing Gehn, enabling Atrus to come here in person; somehow I must locate that Trap Book and recover it.

Having read Atrus's journal, I set out to explore my surroundings. The part of Riven on which I landed was rocky and barren, with only occasional scrubby plants. It appeared that I was on one of a group of islands, with pairs of thick cables running between them—possibly a track for some transport device. Behind my former prison I could see one island with many tall trees to one side, and a large open area where it would appear that a massive logging operation had occurred.

I moved closer to the strange contrivance I'd observed from my prison. The device consisted of an inverted cone suspended above a metal hatch in the ground. I looked into the eyepiece but could see nothing but a white blur. I conjectured that the scope was designed to view that which was below the locked hatch. Curious, I punched buttons randomly for a time, but soon decided that any attempt to unlock the hatch without knowing the combination would be futile. I observed a lever on the supporting structure and a button beneath it, neither of which appeared to have any effect. Perhaps the pipe leading from the contraption into the rocky wall behind me was a conduit for power; perhaps I could discover where the control for that power lay.

The only other item of significance in the immediate vicinity was a large dagger, thrice a man's height, stuck into the ground next to my former prison, which was a surprisingly small building, scarcely big enough for one person to stand in. I examined the lever that my benefactor had employed in releasing me and verified that the mechanism was indeed broken. It gave me great satisfaction to know that no future wanderer would be imprisoned there.

Next, I climbed a series of steps carved into the rock of the hillside. At the top of the steps I had three choices. Ahead of me, stone steps descended to the other side of the hill. To my left I could see past a barren antechamber to a magnificent golden room beyond. To my right a bridge led across a chasm to a doorway into another mountain of rock. Having no idea which way was best, I decided to follow the right-hand path first, setting out across a high and wind-swept bridge that gave me a spectacular view of the sea and my environs. Glancing back, I could now clearly see a titanic dome, gleaming gold in the sunlight, behind and slightly to the left of the rocky prominence around which I had climbed. Ahead, a doorway beckoned in the rock face of a peninsula—almost a small and separate island in its own right.

When I reached the doorway, I could discern steps leading down into the rock. I descended cautiously but encountered nothing sinister. There was a door at the bottom of the steps, massive and stone-hewn. I opened it to find myself in an impressive-looking chamber that resembled nothing so much as a temple, a place of worship. Massive pillars ringed the inside of the chamber. A spherical construction with slender struts like a giant birdcage dominated the front of the room, like some sort of strange, caged altar, immediately before the ornate representation of an enormous, five-armed star that flooded the entire chamber with polychrome light. To either side of the giant cage were statues of large and somewhat sinister looking fish-like creatures, each with paired, out-thrust tusks. Mythical beasts, perhaps? They seemed to have some religious significance, flanking that star-lit altar. In front of each statue were piles of fruit, flowers and other items that I could only deduce were offerings of some kind. From this, as much as anything else, I decided to call it the Temple, and the location Temple Island. Directly opposite the cage was an intricately carved—and solidly locked—door. After an exhaustive and fruitless search for a key or some kind of lock mechanism, I located again the heavy stone door through which I had entered the Temple, inconspicuously set into the wall behind the pillars, and began to climb the steps. It seemed that this path was a dead-end and that enormous golden dome was calling to me now, plucking at my curiosity.

Halfway up the steps, however, I noticed a door to my right and, to my delight, found it unlocked. Through this door was a small room in which was but a single chair, almost a throne, surrounded by a cage of thin struts similar to the one I'd seen in the Temple below. As I approached, the cage lifted, enabling me access to the chair. I sat down and observed some controls on the chair's arms. Pressing the button on the right-hand arm lowered the cage-like structure around me.

I was struck by the resemblance between this structure and the larger one down the steps in the Temple. Directly in front of me was a star-shaped apparatus of some kind, much like a microphone or some sort of visual pick-up. Some kind of broadcasting device, perhaps, a means of projecting a larger-than-life image into the temple cage? There was no visible effect when I moved the lever on the left-hand arm, but I suspected that, had the device been powered, someone in the temple at that moment would have seen my likeness hanging in the star-illumined air between the two fish-beast statues and their offerings. I wondered who it was that used this device, and to what ends. Was it his intent to be worshipped as a god? If so, was he deliberately deceiving the inhabitants, or did he actually think he *was* a god?

In other words, was he vicious… or mad?

It was with some relief that I released myself from the broadcast chair. The thoughts I had been entertaining of the character of its previous occupant were not pleasant. Two additional items in the room had caught my notice. On one wall, to the right of the door through which I'd entered, was a round screen, showing an external view of stone and sea cables. On the other side of the door, a similar screen revealed a view of the Temple, looking down at the locked door. There was a lever on the wall next to the screen. I felt certain that it too would be unpowered, but I tried it nonetheless. To my surprise, I was quite wrong. The image in the viewscreen immediately showed the door lifting and light flooding into the Temple. Racing out of the room and down the stairs to verify my suspicion, I discovered that the image and reality were one and the same; the door was now open!

Beyond the door was the other view I had seen from the broadcast chamber. There were stone steps leading to…nothing. The cables I could now see, appeared to run between this island and one to the south. Perhaps a transport system of some kind? Next to the foot of the steps was a slender pillar topped with a large blue button, possibly a call button. Whether pressing it would call a transport car, I could not tell, but I had no desire to test it as yet. There was much I still had to learn about this island before I ventured beyond it. I would return to the other side of the bridge and investigate the other paths first.

The giant dome called to me.

Upon returning to the bridge I was struck anew by the magnificence of the Great Golden Dome, as I now called it in my mind. I wondered if a way could be found to travel to that Dome from the chamber inside the rock. I was eager to investigate the chamber, but I was also somewhat wary. I decided to exhaust my other options first.

I descended the stairs to the right and found nothing at the bottom but a crude wooden gate with a padlock barring the way into a cave in the mountainside. I searched briefly for a key, but then discovered that I didn't need one, thanks to erosion and my relatively compact size and frame. Inside the cave was a ladder, and there was just enough light for me to see to climb it. At the top I found a peephole through which I could make out a view of the golden room, but there was no apparent way into the chamber from here. I could see a massive pillar straight ahead and a doorway to the right covered by a metal grate. I retraced my steps around to the first entrance, and determined at last to enter the chamber.

The antechamber contained nothing but a single button on the right-hand wall. The chamber itself was pentagonal in shape, with one doorway leading out in the direction of the Great Dome, the same doorway I had seen from inside the cave. Unfortunately that doorway was concealed with a metal grate, intricately worked around the same five-armed symbol I had seen in the Temple. Through the grate I could peer out at the golden brilliance of the Dome beyond the bridge, but there was no visible mechanism that might have caused the grate to open. The remaining three walls were each covered with a strange writing, undoubtedly Rivenese script…

or might it have represented the language of lost D'ni, the fallen civilization so assiduously studied by Atrus and his father Gehn? Remembering the pinhole view I had had of this room from the cave, I looked closely and detected a small hole in each of those walls. What rooms, I wondered, lay behind the other two walls, and how could I reach them?

The five-armed symbol was duplicated on the floor of this gate chamber in a large golden seal. Recalling from Atrus's journal that Gehn called this place the Fifth Age, I wondered if this five-pointed star in the middle of this five-sided chamber was a reference to Riven, or to the one who, as he thought, had created it.

There were five pillars in the room—continuing the pattern of fives—and on each was the three-dimensional, graven image of a large golden beetle. Pulling a ring near a beetle's tail caused the beetle to extend its wings, revealing a small window.

Each window revealed a different image, illumined like a stained glass painting within a peephole set in the beetle's back. Clearly, the images were of a religious nature. The first showed a godlike figure writing in a book, and from the tip of his pen came streams of suns and moons and stars, of animals, insects, and men. Could the ascetic, white-garbed figure represent Gehn?

A second image showed the same godlike figure rising from the sea, with crowds of people kneeling in worship.

The third, I thought, touched on things I previously knew about. Gehn, again, looked on as a small figure and a book tumbled into a fissure filled with stars. That, I knew, was Atrus, and the fall that had been responsible for my finding the Linking Book that had taken me to Myst, and Atrus, in the first place.

A fourth illuminated image within a beetle's back seemed to describe the book-making process itself, with trees being felled, logs being reduced to chips, a large boiler of some kind, and pages being handed to children. I was interested in the presence of five graphic designs composed of tiny squares. What did these represent?

The final image was almost brutally simple: a hand inscribed with a star—the same symbol that decorated the floor of this room—was extending a large book from the heavens down to humans who groveled before it.

With nothing more to examine in the room at present, I returned to the antechamber to see what might result upon pressing the button on the wall.

At first, nothing. Then a harsh grating sound, as of rock against rock, as the room began to rotate clockwise. The far wall disappeared from view as a wall of stone appeared in front of me. When the rotation stopped, I was facing a curved stone alcove where the doorway had been. A peephole in the stone presented me with a view of the room similar to the one I had had from the cave. A fascinating mechanism! Clearly the rotating room with its two offset open doors represented a kind of elaborate gateway puzzle, which, once the pattern was learned and the geometry clear, could afford entrance to any of the inner room's five available doorways. I continued pressing the rotation button and sketching my observations in the journal. Once I deduced the pattern, I determined to see how far I could penetrate this maze.

After rotating the room appropriately, I returned to the cave at the bottom of the northern stairs. As I entered the cave, I was delighted to note that my deductions had been correct. I climbed the ladder to a now-opened door and entered the chamber. The second open door now connected with the wall to the left of the path I'd originally entered the room, and I proceeded to explore this new option.

Beyond the antechamber was a small cave with a tangle of power conduits. One pipe led straight through a hole in the "roof" of this rocky chamber. Another led straight into the rock to my right and I surmised that this was the other end of the pipe I'd noted earlier, connected to the viewing device I had observed outside. The diagram on the upper pipe led me to believe that throwing the lever on the pipe junction would convey power to the mechanism, but since I had, at this time, no idea of the purpose of the device, I decided against empowering it. Returning to the antechamber, I noticed both a rotation button, as I had expected, and a lever, as I had not quite dared hope. It was similar to the one in the temple broadcast room that had raised the door in the temple. If this lever operated similarly, the remaining question was, which grate would it raise? There was but one way to find out.

One of the blocking grates was, indeed, now raised, although the way beyond (through the fourth wall) was still blocked by a heavy door, which also was marked with the five-armed star shape that I now considered to be the symbol of Gehn. The antechamber, however, did contain both a rotation button and a grate lever. If this one didn't succeed, I would have no recourse but to attempt to call the temple transport. My investigations here would be at a standstill.

My excitement was building. As I pressed the button for the final rotation that would, I hoped, open the way for my exploration of the Golden Dome, I felt a shiver of anticipation. What manner of wonders awaited me there?

Yes! The way was free! That last switch I threw had raised the last remaining grate. I crossed the chamber eagerly, noting as I passed that this gateway also had a rotation control. The Great Dome filled the sky in front of me. I was vaguely aware of rocky cliffs to either side and ocean beyond, but my focus was forward. I walked cautiously into the cavernous interior, noting in the doorway a lever to my left but no other obvious controls. The bridge from the Gateway Chamber led directly to a catwalk that extended into the interior and then turned abruptly left and followed the curve of the dome. About a third of the way around the inside of the dome, it descended to a lower level. Before following that path, I examined my immediate surroundings more closely.

Directly in front of me, hanging above the precise center of that vast and cavernous space, was a giant inverted hemisphere with five massive pipes radiating from it in all directions, like the legs of an enormous spider. This structure was suspended from a flat ceiling, perhaps the roof of the dome, or perhaps the floor of a second level. Below, the entire space was filled with steaming, bubbling water, heated, perhaps, by some deep-buried pocket of living magma or subterranean boiling spring.

To my right as I entered the dome, I could see a second catwalk, which started on the opposite side of the dome and stopped some goodly distance shy of what I termed the main catwalk. It appeared to me that the second catwalk was designed to be extended in order to join up with the main catwalk; a wheel was mounted on the railing of the other catwalk that might be the control mechanism, but there was no visible means of getting from where I was to the location of the wheel. I considered trying the lever near the doorway but decided against it. That device seemed likelier to control  some aspect of the bridge or the doorway than the catwalk extension.

One last item of note: a plaque mounted on the main catwalk railing. It appeared to be a representation of the Great Dome, showing the incomplete catwalk encircling a central circle from which extrusions led in each of five different directions. At the end of each extrusion was a different collection of squares, differing both in number and in arrangement. I deduced from this schematic—which I copied carefully into my journal—that the collections of squares represented five buildings or structures of some kind, all of which received power from the same source—this dome. On the other hand, my interpretation of the display could be wildly inaccurate. Perhaps there was a numeric significance to these geometric figures.

Next, I followed the main catwalk clockwise around the interior of the dome and descended, noting as I did so, not only the doorway to which I was headed, but also two other doorways on the upper level leading from the second catwalk. It appeared that if I wished to extend the catwalk, I would need to find another means of entering the Great Dome. On the lower level, a connector catwalk led me to a walkway running clockwise along the outside of the building. From this vantage point I could see clearly that I was, indeed, on an island. Furthermore as I continued along the walkway and looked back, I saw another island to the west with an immense raised drawbridge that would appear, when lowered, to connect with this island. A little further along the walkway, a second walkway extended out over the rocky ground below. At the end of that walkway, a vertical pipe was spewing a great quantity of steam into the air. Another pipe joined it from the west. I determined to take a closer look after I had followed the original path to its end.

Continuing along the main walkway, I noticed something singularly curious ahead: it was a large, fast-spinning dome of some kind. Far smaller than the Great Dome, of which it seemed to be a satellite, it rested at the end of yet another walkway, but I could discern no means of accessing it. I entered a stone tunnel, beyond which the path extended for a short way and then came to an abrupt end at another junction of steam pipes. This appeared to be the power control for a bridge above me, perhaps the very bridge I had crossed from the Gate Room to the Great Golden Dome. I thought again of the lever at the doorway and wondered whether there was a connection here. After some hesitation, I decided to throw the power control lever and return to the bridge to determine if my conjecture was correct.

It was, although to what end, I cannot say. Moving the lever in the doorway caused the Great Dome end of the bridge to rise, thereby trapping me in this building with no discernible means of escape. I was relieved to note that lowering the lever returned the bridge to its original position. I then retraced my steps down the catwalk to the outside walkway.

This time I followed the walkway leading away from the dome. The diagram on the vertical pipe indicated that this control empowered the drawbridge I had observed to the west. At this stage in my explorations it had become obvious that I was going to need to extend my journey to the other islands in this group. Turning on the power for the draw-bridge here might enable a quick return to this island, assuming I were to find myself on the other island at some indeterminate future time. I had no means of verifying the  validity of my conjecture, but I felt that I could do no harm by throwing the switch.

One mystery remained: the small spinning dome on the north coast. There must be a way to get to the dome, but I confess myself perplexed. I had a moment's hope when I noticed a metal panel in the main walkway just before the entrance to the tunnel in the rock, and that hope was intensified upon seeing a button on the wall next to it. Perhaps this was a vertical trans-port device similar to the one I encountered in the Channelwood Age dur-ing my earlier adventures on Myst.

Alas, no. Pressing the button had no effect, and upon stepping back and looking up, I saw a gap in the walkway above me of a size to match my unmoving metal panel. It appeared that it was an elevator, but the controls must be on that upper walkway. Yet another task to await my return to this island from another direction.

It appeared that nothing was left on Temple Island for me to explore, at least nothing to which I could currently gain access. My next step, obviously, was to ride the temple transport car to wherever it would take me. As I retraced my steps through the Great Dome, I thought about my strange benefactor. To what end had he—or she; I could not tell with certainty—taken my book and then set me free? I was assuming, of course, that the guard, if that's what he was, had been under orders from Gehn and that the masked indi-vidual was a member of an opposing faction. If that were so, then what would this mysterious rebel make of the Trap Book? Surely, no one else in this world would recognize a Linking Book or know what to do with it. No one, except… Catherine.

The more I thought about the idea, the more excited I became. This rebel, surely, was my lead to Catherine! I resolved to keep my eyes open for any sign of more of my black-clad allies. If I could locate both Catherine and Atrus's Trap Book, then surely I could contrive a way to keep her safe while

I found and imprisoned Gehn. Then the two of us would be free to signal Atrus and escape this dying world.

My euphoria lasted until I was descending the steps leading to the Temple, whereupon reason caught up with me. I had seen no signs of human habitation, no indications, save the offerings in the Temple, that there was anything or anyone living here at all. And yet I expected, not only to be able to persuade the rebels that I was on their side, but even to *find* the rebels in the first place! What arrogance! If I was to succeed in my quest, I would require not merely all the ingenuity and cunning I possess, but more than that, a healthy dose of luck.

I stood at the foot of the stone steps and gazed out across the sea at the next island to the south. The rightmost half of the island was covered with trees, but the left half appeared quite barren. I found myself quite eager to explore this new and equally mysterious place and pressed the call button with growing excitement. Scarcely had I pressed it when an object detached itself from the distant gloom to fly along the cable connecting that island with this. It slowed as it approached and came to a gentle stop directly opposite the steps. Judging from the way the car hung lightly on the cables, it was propelled by a form of magnetic levitation.

Despite my eagerness, I stepped into the tram car with some slight trepidation. I had become accustomed to unusual means of conveyance during my explorations of Myst, but I anticipated that this tram ride would be unlike anything I had experienced thus far. I sat down in the single chair and examined the controls. As I turned around the car, I said a mental farewell to Temple Island and then set the vehicle in motion. After an agonizingly slow start, the car then picked up speed and whipped me along the tram line with no consideration whatever for the condition of my stomach. I caught fleeting glimpses of other islands as I raced headlong above the ocean, expecting at any moment that I would be plunging into the sea. It took quite a number of heartbeats before I was truly aware that the car had stopped and I was safely at my destination.

But what was my destination? Where had I landed? And what new adventures awaited me here?

Once my stomach returned to its customary position beneath my breastbone and my heart resumed normal operation, I exited the tram and found myself in a narrow sunlit corridor bordered by sandstone cliffs. As I entered the open area beyond the tram station, I was struck by a singular-looking object that appeared embedded in the rock. Upon closer examination, I discovered it to be a brown wooden sphere with a stylized painting of an eye on it. I was drawn to touch it, to see if it had any other function than that of art. It rotated under my fingers, making a chirping sound as it moved and briefly revealing a symbol unknown to me on the reverse side of the sphere before it returned to its former position. What a curious construct! I wondered about its purpose.

Opposite me a stairway had been carved into the rock, leading deep inside the mountain. With occasional glances back at the Eye, I began what promised to be a substantial climb. After perhaps a dozen steps, I turned for one final look at this seemingly useless artifact and, as I did so, was struck by a queer visual effect: the rocks of the tunnel mouth formed the distinct outline of an animal… a frog, I thought! Not only that, the Eye was so placed as to be perceived as the creature's eye. I hastily returned to the Eye and played its music once again. It might have been my imagination—was I now seeing significance in the slightest of coincidences?—but I felt that the chirping sound could in fact be the call of a small frog. With the juncture of the shape in the rocks, the sound of the Eye, and the symbol on its reverse side could it be that the symbol represented the word "frog" in the language of the inhabitants of this place? I made a careful sketch in my journal of the Eye symbol, the frog symbol, and the shape of the frog in the rocks.

Feeling a bizarre combination of satisfaction that I had made a connection and frustration at my inability to make sense of it, I renewed my climb. Eventually I came to an opening in the rock leading to another stone staircase going both up and down. Determined to be systematic in my explorations, I chose the right-hand path, which continued upward. Melodic bird calls and animal chirpings accompanied me on my climb, but there were few visible signs of life. At the top of the cliff I emerged into the logged-out area I had observed from Temple Island. Ahead of me, one path led to a gateway into an area that looked to be more jungle than forest, while another path veered to the left as though to circumnavigate the jungle. I followed the right-hand path until I came to another fork. This branch of the path came to an abrupt stop at a hole in the ground, at the bottom of which could be seen a small cart. Cautiously I got in and found it to be riding on some kind of track, which, taken in conjunction with the lever to my left, led me to believe that it was yet another kind of transport system. Having just made my way to Jungle Island, I felt that the time was a bit soon for me to leave it. Accordingly, I hauled myself out of the cart and continued on the path to the fenced enclosure.

The gate was a simple wooden one, similar to the one in front of the cave on Temple Island, with the singular difference that this gate had no padlock. On the right-hand gate post, I noticed a rather large gold-colored beetle, the living model of the metal insects on the pillars inside the Gate Room. Apparently, the golden color of the carvings showed no artistic license but was an accurate representation of reality. I reached out to touch the beetle, and with a *whirr-click* and a flap of its wings, it flew away. Thus far, this insect and one bird glimpsed in the distance marked the only signs of life I had seen on these islands since my release. Surely *someone* must live here! But where?

I walked through the gate and into a lush jungle. Through the trees I could just make out a spinning dome similar to the one I had seen on Temple Island. Eagerly I pressed forward. When I stopped and turned to obtain a better view of the dome, I noticed yet another immense knife stuck in the ground. I continued downward and onward, the rumble of the spinning dome filling my ears. Passing through a tunnel in a giant tree trunk, I noticed to my left an intriguing species of blue iridescent fungus. I turned to investigate and detected a stone pathway leading down to the base of the giant knife.

Another Eye! I rotated it to hear quite a different sound—something between a roar and a bark—and discovered on its hidden surface a different symbol. I carefully copied down the symbol and described the sound, looking around in vain for its referent. Perhaps the symbol meant "knife" since it was embedded into the base of the knife, but in that case, what was the significance of the sound?

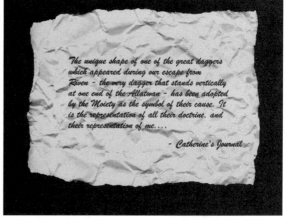

As I returned to the main path, I could see that the spinning dome was at a level above me, with catwalks leading to it. I continued on the path, which led directly into the base of the dome, but I still detected no means of ascending. Underneath the dome, the path forked; following the pattern I had set, I took the right-hand path. As I emerged into the light again, I noticed a webwork of catwalks in the upper tier of the jungle and something that might have been a doorway into a giant tree. Down some more steps and forward brought me face-to-face with an

The unique shape of one of the great daggers which appeared during our escape from Riven - the very dagger that stands vertically at one end of the Atlatwan - has been adopted by the Moiety as the symbol of their cause. It is the representation of all their doctrine, and their representation of me....

- Catherine's Journal

immense statue, an idol of some kind, with orange spotlights wreathing it in a golden glow. With bulbous eyes and extended tusks, it was strongly reminiscent of the fish-like creatures in the Temple and obviously a significant part of the Rivenese mythos. A manifestation of a god, perhaps? Or the god's intermediaries? Whatever they were, I needed a name for them. In terms of size and bulk, they called to mind the great whales, yet something about their expression and the ferocity of those tusks made me think of sharks. Perhaps whark? No, that looked too much like a composite. I decided—in my own mind, at least—to call them wahrks. Somehow, almost mystically, the name seemed to fit.

This appeared to be the end of this path, so I turned and retraced my steps. The spinning dome was frustratingly close, yet like its twin on Temple Island, impossible to access. All I could do was walk underneath it again and take the right-hand path to continue my explorations, hoping that I would have more success in that direction.

But all I saw after emerging from under the base of the dome were steps rising up to another wooden gate. Dejected, I climbed the steps heading out of the jungle. I felt I was making little progress at unraveling the mysteries of Riven. Since my arrival in this Age, I had seen but two human beings. Where were the people who had laid those offerings at the tusks of the wahrks in the Temple? Where *were* they?

As I pulled open the gate, I discovered part of my answer. I emerged out onto a wooden walkway raised above a cavern, and high atop a long pole rising at the side of a cliff was what I can only describe as a guard tower. As soon as I stepped onto the walkway, I observed through a window in the tower what appeared to be an arm turning some kind of crank. Simultaneous with that motion, an object sticking out of the top of the tower began to spin, emitting a low moan or wail as it did so. This continued for a few seconds, after which the arm disappeared, the object ceased spinning, and the moaning stopped. I concluded that the moaning siren was a warning, an alert that a stranger was approaching.

After I verified that the path to my left would return me to the clear-cut area, I proceeded on the right-hand path, which shortly descended on carved stone steps through the rock. Blue lights hanging on the walls illuminated my path, casting an eerie glow on the stone. I could see water below me, through a window in the rock. Looking out, I could see nothing but endless ocean. Perhaps I was descending to a dock or a wharf on the sea, where I might find a calmer mode of transport between islands than the stomach-lurching tram I had employed on my journey from Temple Island.

However, as I continued down the path, I found myself walking a scant few feet above a clear lake that was ringed about by sheer cliffs. To my right I spied a low opening in the rock that might lead to the ocean, but I saw no sign of boats. The cliffs in front of me were dotted with strange spherical constructions, and I could see people scurrying about on a ledge or walkway halfway up one cliff. A child was playing by the water's edge until its mother appeared and spirited it off to safety. I found myself wondering why these people were so reclusive and afraid of strangers. What sort of life did they lead, hidden away here inside this crater lake?

Just off the main dock of this peculiar village, a ladder poked up out of a hole in the water. A hole, a *literal* hole in the water! Surrounding the ladder at a distance of several feet was a sheer, squared-off wall of water behaving in a *most* unwaterlike manner. Was water somehow different in this Age? Or was this evidence of Gehn's sinister manipulations? There appeared to be other "holes in the water" at various intervals scattered about the lake. I would need to investigate further.

As I neared the Cliff Village, more details became apparent, in particular, the remarkable engineering of the roughly spherical, dried-mud structures forming a small town in the sky. The ingenuity of these constructions astounded me, far more so than the outwardly more impressive chambers and domes I had seen on Temple Island, for these were the product of ordinary people, rather than the god or gods of the Temple. I wished I could persuade them that I was their friend.

The path I was on ended at a ladder resting against the cliff. I stood at the base of the ladder, thanking whatever gods there might be that I was in excellent physical condition and that heights had never bothered me. I climbed. After reaching the uppermost platform, I took a moment to survey my surroundings, which appeared stranger and stranger the more I looked. Across from me was a tower-like construction consisting of ropes or cables leading from a decorated crown near the top of the cliff down to a circular platform suspended right at the water's level, next to one of those mysterious holes in the water. A catwalk followed the curve of the cliff wall from the crown around to where it ended abruptly a dozen or so feet above the wooden walkway I had just traversed. A series of tracks crisscrossed the lake bed, apparently connecting these holes. At the base of the cliff to my right was another of those holes, considerably larger than the hole at the Village Dock to my left.

Turning away from the lake, I observed one of these ingenious spherical houses with a board leading directly from the platform where I was standing to its front door. I crossed the board and knocked on the door, using as a doorknocker another of the five-pointed stars that I have come to refer to as Gehn's symbol. A small aperture in the door opened up and a cautious face peered out, a brief glance only, and then I was shut out with a bang. It appeared a direct approach was not going to work with these people.

I followed the path off to the left of this house, emerging at last on the top of the cliff, where I found a conical oven or kiln next to a ceremonial area of some kind, complete with miniature golden wahrk. I have now seen four different representations of this beast, ranging in size from small to enormous. This confirms my suspicion that the creature must be mythical, perhaps a village totem of some sort.

But the most interesting find, from the point of view of my investigations, was what appeared to be yet another transport device, perhaps for traveling through the water along the tracks I had observed on the lake bed. Roughly spherical, bulky, and all of solid iron, the object squatted like a huge, clockwork toy on metal wheels. A lever next to the device would presumably lower it to the large "hole in the water" I had observed at the base of the cliff, but I could see no way in which I could both be in the craft and engage the lever, and if I were to engage the lever before getting into the craft, how would I then be able to enter it? I made careful sketches in my journal, not only of the items on this plateau but also of the view across Village Lake, and then retraced my steps down to the lakeside and out through the tunnel by the sea.

As I emerged from the stone tunnel onto the walkway outside the jungle, I noticed a catwalk above my head crossing from the Jungle to Village Lake. If my assessment of the geometry of the place was correct, this catwalk would emerge above the crater very near the crown-topped platform I had observed from the Submarine Plateau. I reentered the Jungle and confirmed that this catwalk was the same one leading from the spinning dome. At the moment, however, I knew not how to find my way to either place, so my newfound knowledge was not of much use.

I continued up the path to the clear-cut and beyond, across the bridge and down the stone steps. As I passed the entrance to the Temple Island tram, I could see what appeared to be a small lagoon near the ocean's edge. Several large aquatic creatures with extraordinarily long necks were sunning themselves on a rock in the lagoon. I approached slowly, not wanting to startle them. The two beasts raised their heads, snorting and grunting as they caught sight of me, but when I remained still, they calmed down. They were quite large—of no species familiar to me in *my* world—black and white, like enormous penguins. There was something avian about their immense bills, but, unlike birds, they each possessed four paddle-like flippers and a short, lizardlike tail, which made their bodies resemble nothing so much as a member of the long-extinct family of the plesiosaurs. Their bills carried rows of baleen, however, like some whales. I crept yet closer, freezing each time they became aware of me. How close could I get to these magnificent creatures?

When I reached the edge of the lagoon, one of the Sunners raised his head and barked a startling sound. Determined not to disturb them further, I turned and followed the curve of the lagoon to see if I could find another way of approaching them unobserved. As I began to move away, I heard a snort and turned back. The Sunners were gone! They had slipped into the water so quietly I hadn't heard the splash at all. All I saw was a slight ripple in the water marking their passage out to sea. I continued along the beach to where they had disappeared, but there was no further sign of them.

As I returned to my path, I was struck by the shape of a large rock in the middle of the lagoon. It looked like a wahrk! A crude representation to be sure, but unmistakable. I waded across a sandbar for a closer look and found yet another rotating, wooden Eye. The symbol on its reverse side was, to my keen interest, identical to the symbol inside Gehn's five-pointed star. I duly noted it in my journal, along with a description of the sound the Eye made, and I was walking back along the beach when two other sounds I had heard made a connection in my brain; the sound I had heard from the rotating eye in the Jungle was identical to the bark of the Sunners! The symbol on the back of that Eye must refer to these gentle sea creatures, and not to the nearby knife, as I had surmised.

There was a bounce in my step as I returned to the path and followed it deep into the rock. I did not know the significance of the bits of knowledge I had acquired thus far, but I was beginning to make some sense of this Age.

I emerged from a long—fortunately, well-lit—tunnel to find myself on a walkway that I had observed from the Submarine Plateau. There was a guard tower straight ahead of me, but I saw no sign of the guard. From the end of the walkway, I had a clear view of the crown-topped suspension platform

(I must come up with a better name for it); perhaps if I can at some future time utilize the submarine to explore the lake bed, I can approach closer and determine its purpose.

To my left I could see across to Submarine Plateau, but there was a wide chasm between me and the waiting machine. I followed a ladder down to a ledge with a small circular pool, which was completely dry. I could see one pipe leading into the pool, as well as several possible drainage holes. There was also another Eye.

I rotated the Eye and noted the symbol. The sound the eye made was very faint, and I could hardly make it out above the scraping of wood as it turned. As I backed away from the pool, I noticed a petcock off to the side. I turned the petcock and watched the pool fill partway with water. The shape of the water in the pool reminded me of a profile view of an insect, a beetle with a high, rounded back. Yes! Now I had it! I tried the eye again, and this time I recognized the sound, the *whirr-click* of that beetle on the Jungle gate post. Now I had four symbols, sounds, and creatures!

If only I knew what they signified…

With a puzzled sigh, I continued my explorations. On the far side of the pool I had observed a ladder going down, so I followed it. At the base of the cliff, a walkway led into the base of the Submarine Plateau and through the rock to a ladder, similar to the one at the Village Dock. Now I understood! *This* was where I would be able to board the submarine once I returned to the Village and lowered it.

It looked as though I had another long walk ahead of me.

I retraced my steps, up the cliff, through the rock, past the Sunners' lagoon, up the stone steps, through the clear-cut, down into the rock again, around Village Lake, and up to Submarine Plateau. There I threw the lever and lowered the submarine, and then returned all the way around to the Submarine Dock. I was right! The ladder here now allowed me access to the submarine hatch. I was about to embark on an underwater exploration of Village Lake.

It took me very little time to master the controls, considerably longer to explore all possible paths and to be certain of returning to the dock where I had originally entered the craft. The power constraints of the vehicle appeared to be such that it could only travel a very short distance before needing a recharge. The designer had made allowances for this deficiency by designing intermediate stops or junctions along the path. I could have wished he had been a trifle more profligate with his resources and had established a junction between each pair of stops, instead of allowing each junction to serve multiple roles. For a time I was convinced that there were many more junctions than there actually were. But eventually I was able to draw a map that I felt assured was reasonably accurate.

There were five main stops along this submarine path and two junctions, one three-way and the other four-way. At the time I started my explorations, only two of the stops had ladders so placed that I could exit the craft: my starting location, at Submarine Dock, and one other. I disembarked at the other, to find myself faced with a long climb up the cliff face by means of rungs embedded in the rock. I mentioned earlier that I had no fear of heights. Nonetheless there is something disconcerting about clinging to a vertical cliff like an awkward spider clambering up and up and up. The poor spider was forced to take a rest once he reached the top.

A window overlooking the lake afforded me an excellent opportunity to check my map. Well, a cartographer would have laughed me to scorn, but at least the relative positions of the main stops seemed to be correct. On the wall opposite the window was a rack of five levers corresponding, I supposed, to the five sub stops. Two of the levers were in the raised position and three in the lowered. I experimented with the levers for some time, returning frequently to the window to observe the consequences of my actions. It appeared, as I had hoped, that the levers controlled the extending of the ladders above each stop. When I left this Control Room, it was with all five levers raised and all five ladders extended.

At the first junction I encountered upon leaving the Control Room Dock, I took the left-hand fork, emerging in front of a small building. Upon entering the building, I observed benches arrayed in rows and two boards of slate, one filled with writing, attached to the wall at the front of the room. A School Room, then! The sheer familiarity of the setting after so much strangeness nearly made me laugh out loud. Displayed along the wall around the sides of the room were what I took to be individual letters. Six lamps ringed the chamber, each decorated with stylized representations of the mythical wahrk. There was a projection cage in front between the two slate boards. A crank on the side operated the mechanism, which seemed to be a recording of some kind. At least, I *hoped* Gehn was not at that moment broadcasting from the Projection Room in the Temple! Most likely it was a motivational speech of some sort. I could not understand the language he spoke, of course, but he certainly seemed an overbearingly arrogant and patronizing fellow. I was glad not to be *his* student, although I would willingly be Atrus's, if he would take me as such.

One item in the School Room particularly caught my eye. After some experimentation, I determined it to be a device for teaching the numerals 1 through 10, an effective one, to be sure, although I would have preferred a less bloodthirsty one. I sincerely hoped that the image of men being lowered head first over a pit into the jaws of a ravenous beast merely indicated an overworked imagination and was not the representation of a reality familiar to the Village schoolchildren. I found myself wondering at a society that would use such a metaphor for instructional purposes.

But what if it weren't a metaphor? The creature was strangely reminiscent of the wahrk. Perhaps the wahrk was not so mythical as I had thought. Could it be that transgressors in this society were actually… no! It was too horrible to contemplate!

I shuddered and returned to my underwater craft.

I proceeded forward at the junction and was just emerging from my craft when the significance of what I had just learned hit me. I opened my journal to the page where I had marked down the symbols on the undersides of the wooden Eyes I had been encountering all over this island, symbols I had been assuming referred to the objects associated with them. In my haste I had forgotten that the conclusion I had come to earlier was merely a hypothesis, to be discarded the instant contradictory information appeared. Now I saw that those symbols were not names of animals, they were numbers! A series of numbers, in fact 2 through 5. Was there another animal silhouette somewhere on this island, with a 1 behind its Eye? I would have to keep my eyes out for it.

And I would have to remember to keep my brain in gear, as well.

The place where I had emerged was directly across Village Lake from the Submarine Dock. I had an excellent view of the Cliff Village from here, as well as of a strange construction in the middle of the lake, which looked like some sort of lens, possibly a camera lens or telescope, extending from a circular base that seemed designed to rotate. Did Gehn spy on his people with this device? Was it possible he might see me? The lens was pointing away from me at the moment, a circumstance for which I was profoundly grateful.

I turned away from my speculations and crossed to the suspended circular platform whose purpose I had been unable to guess before. Perhaps now I could satisfy my curiosity, hoping, of course, to do so in a way that would further my investigations.

The platform consisted of a circular walkway ringing a central opening and connected by spokes to the outer rim. From the cliff side of the walkway I could reach a handle that was hanging by a rope from the apex of the tower. I pulled the handle and watched with some trepidation as a bar descended on a rope from the top of the tower, dangled above the water for perhaps 10 seconds, and then was retracted. With dawning horror I pulled the handle again, seeing in my mind's eye a villager—perhaps one who had dared express an opinion of his own—being lowered, inverted and screaming, over the watery chasm to the waiting jaws of a not-so-mythical beast. The School Room toy did not represent an imaginary punishment for wayward school-children, it was an accurate picture of a day-to-day reality for these virtually enslaved creatures, a place of execution for those who dared dissent!

Hastily leaving the Wahrk Gallows, as I now termed it, I traveled forward to the three-way junction and then took the right fork, emerging at the Village Dock. I turned and deliberately faced the Camera, putting all the detestation and revulsion that I felt into my expression. As useless a gesture, no doubt, as a Beetle threatening a Wahrk, but a satisfying one, somehow.

I seemed to be at a dead end with regard to my explorations of Village Lake, indeed with regard to my explorations of the whole of Jungle Island. There was more to be discovered here, certainly, but at this point I felt certain that only by way of one of the

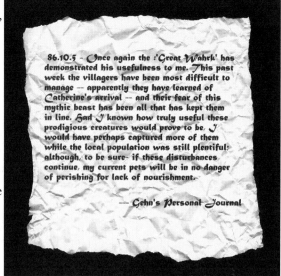

86.10.5 - Once again the 'Great Wahrk' has demonstrated his usefulness to me. This past week the villagers have been most difficult to manage — apparently they have learned of Catherine's arrival — and their fear of this mythic beast has been all that has kept them in line. Had I known how truly useful these prodigious creatures would prove to be, I would have perhaps captured more of them while the local population was still plentiful; although, to be sure- if these disturbances continue, my current pets will be in no danger of perishing for lack of nourishment.

— Gehn's Personal Journal

other islands would I be able to gain access to the areas that were currently hidden from me. Accordingly, I braced myself and prepared for yet another heart-stopping ocean crossing. Submarine travel was slow and tedious, but at least it had the advantage of leaving my stomach where it belonged!

I returned to the clear-cut outside the Jungle and looked out over the sea. The tramway I had used in my journey from Temple Island was clearly visible, as was the drawbridge leading from Temple Island to yet another island. From that island, I saw another tramway, shrouded in sea haze and leading to an unknown destination that was blocked from my view by the trees of the Jungle. I could see no indication of where this logging car might take me—possibly it was merely a subterranean transport to another part of the island I was on. I would soon find out.

I climbed into the car, braced myself as best I could, and threw the lever. The car creaked slowly along the track but very quickly picked up speed as it descended through the earth. I thought I was prepared for anything, but nothing could have readied me for this experience: first plunging precipitously into a cavern hewn through living rock, then through rings of fire that cast a golden glow on the rock walls, then out into the ocean with the same golden rings somehow holding the sea at bay, creating a tunnel underneath the water. The lumber car slowed down as it emerged from the ocean still some distance from the island that was its destination—possibly the one across the drawbridge from Temple Island—and then plunged into utter darkness as it penetrated the side of a mountain. Ahead a small glimmer of light appeared, then grew; the car slowed again to round a final curve, and it stopped with a gentle bump, still inside the mountain. I scarcely had time to notice the platform and steps to my right, however, when the car tilted forward, dumping me down a chute and through a hole in the rock wall. I emerged into daylight, on the shore of a lake surrounded by high vertical cliffs, yet another crater lake. It seemed that while Jungle Island had a large crater in its interior, this island consisted of little more than the crater. Perhaps I should call it Crater Island.

Turning to see where I had exited the mountain, I noticed two hatches, one debouching in the chute down which I had slid. A ladder flush with the cliff face led up to the second hatch, which gave access, no doubt, to the steps I saw while I was still inside the mountain. I had little enough inclination to repeat that tortuous ride, but it was good to know that there *was* a way back, in case I found myself frustrated at another dead end.

I hauled my bruised body out of the metal container into which I had been so unceremoniously deposited and examined my surroundings. A pile of sawdust and wood chips strewn out on the ground beneath me led me to believe that I had been fortunate to have landed at a time when the mechanism was not operational; my conjecture was that its purpose was to masticate the logs transported here from Jungle Island.

This island, or at any rate this part of the island, did not appear to be inhabited. Rather it looked to be the home of some sort of engineering concern. There were a number of pipes coming from a central point in the lake, as well as a long walkway leading out to it. To my right I could see where one of the pipes terminated at a squat, round building of some sort, and I resolved to investigate it further.

It was a circular structure made of brick, with a metal staircase going up to a heavy door and a metal walkway curving around the side. The door was locked, a red light to the side giving warning, and I could feel considerable heat emanating from the structure. Obviously I could not examine the interior in its current condition.

As I followed the outer walkway around the curve of the building, I noticed, farther along the beach, a tall ladder set into the cliff. I sighed. Somehow I knew I would end up having to climb it. I wondered if a fear of heights could be engendered, through repeated exposure, in an previously fearless individual.

At the side of the circular building I came across a Y-shaped pipe, the stem originating in the middle of the lake and the two forks of the Y leading to the building controls. The valve was pointed down the left-hand fork, which led past a large wheel with a hand crank. A long slit of a window revealed boiling water within the tank. A lever to my right was pointing along a pipe heading straight into the building. I raised it to the upright position and was rewarded with growing silence as the furnace ceased its roaring and the water stilled. I returned to the door to discover that the red light was now off and the door unlocked.

A glance at the interior of the structure revealed a central ladder extending down into the water, which was almost to the level of the door. The floor was far below me, but there were metal protrusions around the sides, stuck into what might have been tracks, that made me think it was a kind of platform, capable of being raised and lowered, rather than a floor. Light entered the chamber through a series of round holes high up in the wall.

Returning to the side of the building, I examined the controls once more. I turned the wheel and was treated to the sight of the section of large pipe to which it was attached breaking away and rotating in my direction. However, to my surprise that action had no effect on the level of water in the tank. From the size of the pipe I felt it might be a water pipe. I explored around the base of the building to discover that both the main pipe and a second pipe like it came directly out of the lake. The main pipe curved sharply upward to join with the accordion section of pipe that I had rotated out of the way. The second pipe ran under the building where it seemed to join with another, even larger pipe that came down from the middle of the building, led off along the shore, and then turned to climb the cliff.

I then restored the accordion pipe to its original configuration, reset the valve to the right-hand fork, and raised the handle on the wall. No effect whatsoever. I lowered it again.

My next stop was undoubtedly the construction in the middle of the lake.

At the end of the walkway I came to a small stone bollard with four pipes leading out of it. Three of the four appeared to be controlled by a valve on top of the bollard. I turned the valve so that it pointed in the direction of the circular building, thus—I hoped—turning on the power to the boiler controls. As I started back along the walkway, I noticed where the ladder further down the beach ended—at a balcony with an elaborate entrance. Somehow I felt certain I would be climbing that ladder before long.

I was right. With the power being funneled from the center of the lake, the boiler controls were now operational. I set the valve along the left-hand fork, rotated the pipe, and watched delightedly as the water level in the tank fell. I ran to the door again and confirmed that the water had receded, but that the ladder was still inaccessible. I then reset the valve to the right-hand fork and raised the handle on the wall. With a grinding creak the floor raised up, and when I returned to examine the interior of the tank, I found that I could walk out onto the grating and peer down the ladder to a pipe below me.

It was possible that my destiny lay in following that pipe to its source, but I was inclined to put off that destiny as long as possible. Faced with the prospect of descending into a dark and damp pipe with no notion of where it led, I suddenly felt less uneasy at the idea of climbing a ladder, no matter how tall, in broad daylight. Accordingly, I walked down the beach to the base of the ladder and started to climb. As I approached the top of the ladder, I could see a hatch set in the floor of the balcony. I prayed fervently that it be unlocked.

My prayers were ignored. This path, at least, was a decided dead end.

As I returned along the beach toward the boiler, I had a clearer view of where that water pipe led. After following the curve of the beach for a time, it angled sharply and climbed the side of the mountain. Perhaps it could take me where I needed to go. I reentered the boiler, climbed down the central ladder, and began crawling in a general southerly direction. In moments it was pitch black, and I had only the sense of touch to rely on. After a considerable time, I detected a trace of, not light, but a lessening of the darkness ahead of me. The not-darkness grew, revealing a curve in the pipe and a ladder slanting upward to a small circle of daylight above. As a moth to a candle, I was drawn to that light.

At the top of the ladder I found myself overlooking sea and sky, a magnificent vista. When I looked down, I could judge how high off the ground I was by the shadow of the pipe. I would have to drop out of the pipe; there was no way to climb down. As I dropped, I hoped I would be able to find a path off this mountain; somehow I doubted I would be able to return to the beach the way I had come. Looking back up at the pipe, I felt certain I would need another path.

I was not quite at the top of the ridge, but the crest was but a dozen or so feet from me. As I reached the crest, I was momentarily awestruck by the spectacle before me. The lake was very far below me. On the far side, I could see the log chipper that was my entrance to this island. And beyond, gleaming in the sunlight and towering over its surroundings, was the Great Golden Dome.

Exploring the paths around me I soon found myself looking down on the balcony I had been unable to reach before. The first thing I did was to unlock the hatch that had prevented my accessing this balcony before. Now I was certain of at least one way down this mountain, although I fervently hoped I could find an alternative.

I was examining the layout of this island from a unique perspective. I could see the power pipes leading out from the central bollard in the middle of the lake and follow their paths to their destinations. The first one led to the log chipper, where I had been introduced to this charming locale. The second led to the boiler, and the third entered the rock below me and to my right. A fourth pipe, the one that was not affected by the power valve, appeared to lead quite a ways off to my right. I could not see where it ended.

Turning away from the lake with some slight trepidation, I tested the doors set into the face of the cliff. To my relief they opened easily, depositing me on a metal walkway leading deep into the mountain. The path was reasonably well lit, so I had no difficulty following it to its terminus just below the access to a ventilator shaft. The grate was down and I could see and hear the fan turning. Set into the end of the walkway was a puzzling contraption that appeared to be some kind of trap device. A spherical metal ball opened at a touch, revealing a pressure plate inside. To the right of the device was a small tray of food pellets. Feeling reasonably assured that a device of this size could not entrap anything dangerous, I baited the trap and lowered it into the cavern below.

It took me several tries to get the hang of it, but eventually I raised the trap to find it closed. I opened it cautiously and, to my delight, discovered a small frog, glowing with iridescent colors, like a tiny, living jewel. He glanced at me briefly, gave a small chirp, and then jumped out of the trap. That sound! It was the same sound I had heard from the first wooden Eye, confirming in my mind that the symbol I had noticed on the obverse of the Eye, which I now knew to be the numeral 3, was in some way associated with this Rivenese creature. For what purpose I had yet to determine, but I made a notation in my journal nonetheless.

At this point there was nothing more to be done here. I climbed on top of the trap to see if I could reach the ventilator shaft, which I could, but I detected no means of turning off the fan. No escape for me in this direction. I appeared to be at a dead end on this island. I could see no alternative other than descending the ladder to the beach and entrusting myself to a repetition of the logging car ride. I stood out on the balcony for a moment considering my options, which seemed minimal at the moment. There *must* be another way! I could see another catwalk clinging to the side of the mountain and an ornate building beyond. But how to get at it? There *must* be another means of access!

I walked inside the cave once more and turned to examine the doors. Perhaps… ah-ha! A devious fellow, this Gehn. So that's how he hides them.

I first took the passageway to the left, winding down a long flight of steps, emerging at last into a surprisingly light chamber, since it was open to the sky above, in front of yet another spinning dome. Finally. I could see one up close! There seemed to be symbols inscribed on the side of the dome, although the dome was rotating too fast for me to be certain of their design. One of the symbols, presumably one with some special significance, appeared to be marked in yellow. There was a pathway around to the left of the dome, but following it yielded nothing more than a better view of a pipe behind it.

There was nothing more to be done here. It was so frustrating. At last I was face-to-face with one of these enigmatic artifacts, but with no more useful information than I had already possessed.

Dejected, I ascended the stairs proceeding through the tunnel on the other side, and emerged into daylight again on a long catwalk leading to the ornate structure I had noted before and beyond it to a doorway in the cliff. The building, which had a curiously modern feel, all glass, low ceilings, and angles, had large, transparent windows through which I could detect laboratory apparatus of some sort. Because the room appeared to be unoccupied, I tried the door, but found it locked.

I then proceeded along the catwalk to the cliff doorway and followed a tunnel through the rock and out onto a drawbridge with the Great Golden Dome straight ahead of me. This was the bridge I had seen before from the catwalk outside the dome. I crossed the bridge, eager to see if it was in fact this bridge to which I had turned on the power. After walking a long way, I discovered that what I had thought was a drawbridge was in fact an angled extension of the bridge. If it wasn't a drawbridge, I wondered as I climbed the extension, then what was the purpose of the power valve I turned on?

I soon found out. It *was* a drawbridge after all, but the raised section was much smaller than I had imagined, much closer to the Golden Dome, and out of sight of the power valve catwalk. I pushed the lever that I found on the right at the spot where the bridge was raised, and was delighted to see that my original deduction had been correct in kind, although not in location. As the bridge section lowered, I could see that it was going to provide a pathway directly into the Great Golden Dome, probably through one of the doorways I had spotted during my earlier excursions. This, then, was the

return path I had been seeking. Perhaps now I would be able to find a way to Temple Island's spinning dome.

The bridge led onto a catwalk directly opposite the main entrance to the dome from the Gate Room and directly above the lower level entrance. I followed the catwalk around to the left, past one doorway that I resolved to investigate later, and to the end of this section of catwalk. As I had expected, turning the wheel extended the catwalk underneath my feet to meet with the main catwalk ahead of me. I crossed to the main catwalk in great excitement. Although I had not yet explored them as fully as I wished, I had now completed a circuit of three of the islands!

I now had a notion of where the remaining doorway on the interior catwalk would lead me…assuming that the elevator controls were where I had conjectured. Accordingly, I raised the bridge control lever by the main entrance and returned to that doorway to test my hypothesis. As I approached the upper level catwalk, I could clearly see the missing panel, and I could look down and see the lower level where I had failed to activate the elevator. From this vantage point, I could also see a stairway leading up from below that lower level and out to the mysterious spinning dome. Turning back toward the entrance from which I had emerged, I saw what I had been hoping would be there, but as relief washed over me, I realized how uncertain I had been. I pressed the button and saw to my delight the missing panel restored from beneath. The way was now clear to proceed on this outer catwalk.

As I had hoped, the path ended at a solid door with a lever to the right. I raised the lever and found myself inside position 4 of the Gate Room. A few rotations of the chamber enabled me to ascend the raised bridge to the uppermost level of the Great Golden Dome. The ingeniousness of Gehn's constructions almost made me admire the man, although my knowledge of his cruelties enabled me to maintain my focus on what had to be done.

The upper level consisted merely of a long corridor open to the sky leading to a peculiar construction in the middle of the dome. I lowered a lever to my right, revealing a white button and also lowering the mechanism in front of me. Pressing the button had no discernible effect, so I raised the mechanism again and approached it more closely.

The base of the device appeared to be a five-by-five grid of twenty-five squares, each of which was divided into a smaller grid of twenty-five holes. To the right were arrayed six different colored marbles: red, orange, yellow, green, blue, and violet. Undoubtedly, arranging the marbles in a particular configuration upon the grid was the key to the operation of this device, but I was at a total loss as to what that configuration might be. There was a significantly higher probability that I would be able to guess the locking code for the telescope hatch than that I would come upon the correct arrangement of marbles in this grid by random selection.

There was one more area to investigate on this island, and now that I had raised the elevator, I had hopes that my way would be clear to do so. Accordingly, I navigated the Gate Room to place myself once more on the outer catwalk. Returning to the inside of the Great Golden Dome, I followed the interior catwalk around past the main entrance, down to the lower catwalk, and around the outside of the building again. I wasn't sure exactly what I was expecting to find, now that the metal panel had been raised—perhaps a ladder going down—but what I found was that the metal panel that should now have been missing was still there! I was momentarily flummoxed…until I looked up and saw the "missing" panel exactly where it belonged, in the upper catwalk. What would happen now, I wondered, if I were to stand on the lower panel while someone on the upper pressed the elevator button? What would happen…if I pressed the elevator button, the one on this level that I thought didn't work?

I pressed the button and was rewarded with a deep rumbling sound and a light feeling in my gut as I descended to yet a still lower level. Emerging at the bottom of the shaft, I passed through a stone tunnel, up a metal staircase, and along another walkway to the spinning dome. The series of symbols inscribed on the side of the dome appeared to be identical to those on the only other dome I had thus far been able to examine closely, though the one marked in yellow was, I was fairly sure, different. A look through the kinetoscope that was set up on the walkway, aimed at the dome, confirmed my impression that the symbols were variations on a basic circle shape. What would happen, I wondered, if I were to press the button on the top of the kinetoscope simultaneously with the appearance of the yellow symbol?

Whatever I imagined bore no relationship to the reality whatsoever. When I was finally successful in matching the timing of my action with that of the symbol, the rotation of both the dome and the kinetoscope slowed in synchronicity. Once they had both stopped, the yellow symbol was clearly visible, and I resolved to copy it down in my journal. Before I could set pen to

parchment, however, I was transfixed as I watched the dome roll backward to reveal another dome beneath it, this one polished as smooth as any marble and gleaming with a golden fire.

In the center of the Fire Marble, as I elected to call it, I observed a transparent window and another combination lock. Through the window I could look down and see a book…possibly a Linking Book. The locking device consisted of five sliders capable of being moved across a bar marked in five groups of five, and a button beneath the slider bar. I conjectured that once the sliders were arranged in the appropriate configuration, pressing the button would open the window and allow access to the Linking Book…if that's what it was. I tried a number of combinations but with no more success than I had enjoyed at the Telescope Hatch.

I wanted to note the symbol on the Fire Marble Dome in my journal, but I was uncertain I was remembering it correctly. I returned to the kinetoscope, wondering if I could repeat the process. As I had hoped, pressing the button restored the dome to its original state, and pressing it once more enabled me to fix the symbol in my memory. As I copied it down in my journal, I pondered whether I should leave the Fire Marble Dome in its open or spinning state. I was leaving a trail behind me of flipped levers and pressed buttons, but they were not so blatant an advertisement of my presence as this. Having verified that I could open or close the dome at will, I decided that it would be wiser to leave it closed. If Gehn had been nearby, he would have had an audible indicator of my activity, but if not, he still might return to witness my handiwork. Having once escaped his clutches—I presumed it was he who had caused my imprisonment when I first entered this Age—I did not wish to chance repeating the experience. I could not count on the beneficence of a stranger to free me a second time.

There was a lilt in my walk as I retraced my steps. I now felt certain that continued determination would eventually yield all the answers I required. There were islands left to explore, but on this island all that remained was that puzzling contraption on the upper level of the Great Golden Dome, the grid with the six marbles. Undoubtedly more clues would be uncovered in the course of my further investigations.

Marbles. I wondered. Could the arrangement of marbles in the grid have anything to do with the locations of the Fire Marble Domes? I had thus encountered three of the structures, one on each island I had visited. I was convinced that the fourth island, which I could see to my left as I traversed the drawbridge once more, was home to yet another such device. But there

were six marbles. Did that mean there were two additional islands in this
island group, perhaps hidden from view behind one of the others, perhaps so
small or so far away as to be invisible from my current vantage point? Since
I could determine no method of testing my conjecture, I had to content
myself with noting the possibility in my journal. Once I completed my
investigations of the third island, I would turn my attention to the fourth,
which was, I was relieved to note, connected by mag tram with the others.
Perhaps there I would find some additional answers.

Passing through the tunnel in the rock, I came once again to the building I
was terming in my mind Gehn's laboratory, with no better idea of how to
access it than I had had from the start. I would examine the area more closely later, but first I had an appointment with the spinning dome under the
mountain. Now that I knew that the devices could be opened, I was determined to open each one I found. Examining the interior of the chamber
once more, I noted what might have been a lens buried in the rock to the
left of the dome, but could detect no means of accessing it. I returned to the
doorway, wondering. Perhaps if I closed the door… yes! He'd pulled the
same trick here he'd used at the top of the stairs. Following the tunnel in the
rock I soon came to the kinetoscope, employed it to open the dome, and
noted the yellow symbol in my journal. Then I returned to the main cavern
and examined the opening. As with the Fire Marble Dome on Temple
Island, this dome was protecting what appeared to be another Linking Book.
And as before, access to the book was further guarded by a locking device.
While I was no further along in solving this particular puzzle, I felt I was
making progress. I had detected patterns in Gehn's constructions and in his
manner of building. If the Powers overseeing this universe granted me the
time, I felt certain I could unravel this mystery.

Flushed with success, I returned to the outer catwalk and began to explore
more carefully the path between the balcony and Gehn's laboratory. As I did
so, I noticed a wire strung along the side of the cliff. At the laboratory end
it disappeared into the side of the building at the junction of what appeared
to be a large ventilation pipe, perhaps the same ventilation shaft that I had
observed above the trap mechanism. This was indeed promising! I followed
the wire along the cliffside to where it ran up and over the cliff, quite near
the entrance to the frog trap tunnel. Retracing my steps carefully, I examined
every inch of the wire, discovering to my delight a power valve directly
opposite the fourth pipe. A loud sound, as of turning fans, was emanating

from the rock. When I turned the power valve, the sound—no doubt coming from an exhaust vent—stopped. If this action had accomplished what I hoped, I would now have access to the laboratory.

Yes! I returned to the tunnel, climbed on the frog trap, and entered the ventilation shaft. A relatively short crawl found me looking down onto a laboratory desk. After listening carefully for other occupants of the room, I pushed the grate out and lowered myself down to the desk.

Like the Gate Room, this chamber was pentagonal. As I looked about the room, I pondered about the significance to Gehn of the number 5. So many things seemed to come in fives in this world.

I opened the door to the outer catwalk to make sure I wouldn't have to use the ventilator shaft mode of travel again. The other door probably led to the tram I had observed from the drawbridge, but I decided to examine the laboratory thoroughly before I followed that route.

The desk I had landed on contained a number of objects of interest, most prominent of which was Gehn's lab journal. I knew I didn't dare remove it from this place, so I perused it carefully, marking down in my journal those items I felt most noteworthy, such as the D'ni's interest in the number 5 and their color symbology. I wondered if the six colors referred to were the colors of the six marbles I had seen in the upper level of the Great Golden Dome. I was interested to have my idea of Catherine's involvement with the rebel Rivenese confirmed. I was more certain than ever that locating the Moiety, as they seemed to be called, was the key to one half, at least, of my mission—finding Catherine. A reference in the journal seemed to indicate that the Moiety had access to a different Age, where they obtained the strange metal for their knives, perhaps an Age Catherine had written for them?

But the most significant item in the journal was the code to open the Fire Marble Domes, which were designed to connect the islands of Riven with a new Age that Gehn has written. It appeared to be a five-digit code. The only problem was that I didn't recognize all of the digits from the counting game in the School Room. The numbering system appeared combinatory in some fashion. It looked as though I would have to extrapolate from the numbers I already knew, and deduce how the pattern continued.

But not while I was still trespassing on Gehn's property.

One other item of note on the desk: the missing wooden Eye, the Eye with the number one on one hemisphere. A note beside it indicated that Gehn had only recently become aware of these artifacts and, furthermore, that the villagers—or someone—had replaced within a few days of its removal by Gehn. If he were not responsible for the placement of these objects, then who? Could it be the rebels? Could these Eyes provide some sort of clue as to the whereabouts of the rebels' hideout? If the series in fact stopped at the number 5—as seemed likely, given the local preoccupation with that number—then all I was missing was the identity of the creature associated with the number one. Perhaps if I could find the survey room to which Gehn referred…

I gave the rest of the room a hasty inspection, being not at all anxious to be caught here by the precipitous return of the owner. The lamps over each of three desks were all decorated with what looked to be wahrk tusks. I wondered if they shed their tusks, the way deer shed their antlers, or if each pair of tusks represented a wahrk killed. A strange man, this Gehn. He feeds his prisoners to the wahrks and then kills the wahrks for their tusks.

A second table was littered with chemical apparatus and a number of preserved frogs—or ytrams, as Gehn refered to them in his journal—in glass bottles. The journal intimated, and I now saw corroborative detail of the fact, that Gehn utilized these innocent creatures to prepare a smoking extract for his pipe! Disgusting!

It was when I saw the items on the third desk that I finally began to piece together what I had seen into some kind of coherent framework. A massive logging operation on Jungle Island. A transport system designed to carry the logs to this island. A mechanism to chip those logs into fragments. A boiler to reduce those chips to a paste. And in this laboratory, a slab of wood under a microscope. A book in the process of being bound. A book press. It all added up to one thing: Gehn was turning these islands into a factory for producing paper and assembling books!

Fortunately, not all of his attempts had been successful. I smiled as I noticed the charred remnants of one of his failures smoldering in the stove in the center of the room.

Gehn is making and writing Books!
I wish they had told me sooner.
Atrus should have realized this would happen: of course Gehn would have written all of the materials necessary to the D'ni craft of making books into this Age. and probably every other Age he ever wrote.
He is attempting to write his way out of here! We did not imprison him, we only delayed him! This Age has become his factory. and the people are his machines - - all laboring in his mad pursuit to become a god! . . .

-- Catherine's Journal

Enough of this. I'd best leave before Gehn took it into his head to revisit his laboratory. There were two doors to this room, the front door leading to the catwalk outside, and another which headed in the direction of the tramway to the next island. I could sense nothing further to be discovered on Crater Island, so I exited through the back door and descended the stairway to the tram station.

No tram. There was not a call button here next to the steps, as there had been on Temple Island. I searched the immediate vicinity to no avail, but then I remembered something I'd overlooked inside the lab. I returned to the lab and pressed the blue knob by the front door, then retraced my steps down to the tram station.

The rapid response of these devices is impressive. By the time I had retraced my steps down to the station, the tram was there. As I got in and rotated the craft, I discovered that I was actually almost looking forward to the ride. My change of heart was no doubt due to my reluctance to endure a repetition of my imitation of a cart full of inanimate logs.

Someday, perhaps, I will become fully accustomed to this stomach-twisting carnival ride that seems to be the primary form of inter-island transport. I may have to, out of sheer self-defense. I have never cared for roller-coasters and similar forms of so-called amusement, and these dizzying swoops across the surface of the sea were disconcerting in the extreme.

It was with some relief then that I felt the tram slowing, drawing to a halt at last within one of the characteristic massive, hewn-stone docks or stations for these devices. I was interested to note, as the tram swayed to a stop, that although the tram's doorway opened onto a platform to the left of the car, as usual, there was another platform to the right… and a waiting door.

Curious. There seemed to be no way to get over there, however, short of scrambling across the groove within which the tram itself hung from its cables, and I was unwilling to try that. *My* world had subways, commuter train tracks, and electric trolleys, and I certainly didn't fancy having come this far to accidentally electrocute myself on some guide rail or power line in a device still completely alien to my understanding!

That particular mystery could wait for a later opportunity. For now, there was quite enough to occupy my attentions on the platform to the left of the tram. A door leading into a smooth-walled tunnel, and a stairway rising from the end of the tunnel like a kind of fire escape, beckoned to me.

I emerged on an open plateau ringed with, of all things, wahrk tusks. My god, how many of the things had that monster killed? Ahead, though, a new site drew me forward, and my jaw dropped with the stunned wonder of that panorama, a sight that I shall never forget for as long as I draw breath. Monoliths, like titanic crystals hewn from basalt, grew like a gray forest from the algae-clogged pools of water before me, rising, not upright, but at angles from the pond, like some incredible explosion frozen in solid stone. As I drew closer, following a path that wove in among the standing stones, I wondered if what I was seeing was a natural formation of some kind—surely it pointed to some ancient, volcanic cataclysm of world-shaking dimensions—or if it were, instead, a mingling of art and architecture and engineering on a truly godlike scale.

At one point, the metal path spanned a circular opening in the pool through which I could see another pool of some kind underground, orange lit and embraced within some kind of pentagonal structure. Clearly, there were mysteries below ground and above, enough mysteries to keep me busy for quite some time to come.

I continued walking. Dwarfed to insignificance by the sheer grandeur of that stone array, I kept pushing ever onward. Beyond the monoliths, the top of the plateau opened up like the top of a table, flat as the slide resting on the stage of a microscope, with me, an indistinguishable speck, an amoeba, a microbe crawling ever steadily forward. Ahead of me rose what at first I thought were fortress walls, steep, sheer, slightly curved and leaning inward, yet on a scale that would have dwarfed even the most cyclopean earthly structures. A tall and narrow slit in the outer wall swallowed the path, leading upward on yet more steps, and I followed.

It was not a fortress, as I'd supposed. There were no ramparts, no battlements. Instead, the path now ran along a kind of irregular trench with walls a few feet high. To either side was a shallow pool of water, pale green-blue and sparkling in the sunlight. Curious stone shapes rose like plateaus carved from solid rock to either side, and something about them made me think of islands, steep-sided, water-worn, with vertical cliffs for shores, rising from a gentle sea. Each of those "islands" was nearly as big as a house, however, and far too high for me to see their tops.

And still I continued my march. Ahead was yet another cliff, and I could perceive here the hand of man. A structure of some sort—I could not make it out; a telescope? The handle of another titanic dagger?—emerged from the cliff face near the top a hundred feet above my head, secured by massive chains. Just below this enigmatic structure, a kind of catwalk or balcony extended from the mountainside.

My path led into another cleft in the rock, and there I found what was obviously an elevator car. I pushed the button and felt myself start to rise.

At the top I had a choice.

The elevator, it seemed, was open in two directions, although that had not been clear at the bottom. Ahead of me, back the way I'd come, was a path leading a short distance toward an iron railing; in the opposite direction, however, the natural crevice in the rock opened on some stranger, less identifiable structure, squat and reddish in color.

I decided to proceed forward, however, and check the railing. I stepped forward… and nearly fell!

I have said before this that I have a good head for heights, although my continued adventures with tall and spindly ladders had begun sapping some of my confidence in this regard. The view from that overlook, however, made me grasp the iron railing with tightly gripping, white-knuckled fingers, and I found myself drawing a deep breath to steady the swimming sensation in my head.

Slowly, I made myself look, keeping my gaze locked on the far horizon until the vertigo left me. Interesting. From here I had an absolutely spectacular view of the sea beyond this island, and of the other three islands I'd visited as well. I was able to confirm that two tram lines extended across the sparkling water from this island, one—the one I'd just traveled—following a gentle arc back to Crater Island and Gehn's mountaintop lab, the other apparently linking this island with Jungle Island. I reasoned that that must be the way to those parts of Jungle Island that I had not yet explored. Beyond, the Great Golden Dome rose like an impossible, gleaming moon above the irregular outline of Temple Island. From here, the Golden Dome reminded me forcibly of the far smaller Marble Domes, after they'd been opened and their fire-gold interiors revealed. What was the connection, I wondered?

Finally, I had control enough of my heart and stomach to hazard dropping my eyes to the spectacle spread beneath my tiny, cliffside eyrie. I must have been a hundred feet above the shallow pool I had noted earlier upon my approach. I was now looking down on that pool and on five distinct islands rising from the water. The tops of those islands, I could see now, appeared perforated by patterns of holes or drains of some sort laid out in regular lines and columns like a grid. The shapes of the islands were once regular and

naturally rugged. The arrangement of their shapes tugged at my memory. What was it about those shapes?

Affixed to the railing between my white-knuckled hands was a small, brass plate, a rectangle divided into five irregular but rectilinear parts. There was a square at the upper left, an L-shape beneath that, the two fitting like squared-off jigsaw pieces into two larger and somewhat more irregular pieces, with a fifth, a tiny square, at the upper right.

I looked from the plate to the island-plateaus below. Yes! The shapes matched! That lone island off to the right was small, like the lone square on the upper-right corner of the plate. The L-shape was there, and the larger square…

Hesitantly, I reached down and touched the largest section on the plate, the piece corresponding, as I now thought, to the largest of the island plateaus. Immediately, a strange transformation was worked upon the plateau so far below my overlook; water came flooding in through those holes I'd noticed, but like the water of the lagoon back on Jungle Island, this water was not the well-behaved and gravity-minded stuff I knew and remembered from home! Somehow, by contrivance or black art or the alien physics of this universe, the water piled itself up within the third dimension, flowing into distinct mounds and draining from valleys, literally growing a watery representation of mountain peaks right before my astonished eyes.

And I recognized the place.

Yes, I was sure of it now. I could easily make out the circular form of the crater ring, the central hollow representing the lake at the center. That island

plateau represented in startling detail a real island—
Jungle Island, to be precise. Even without the water-
formed mountains, the island was recognizable
from the off-center hole representing Village Lake;
with the mountains in place, the resemblance was
unquestionable.

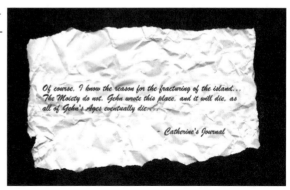

Of course, I know the reason for the fracturing of the island...
The Moiety do not. Gehn wrote this place, and it will die, as
all of Gehn's Ages eventually die...

— Catherine's Journal

I tried another button on the brass plate, the
L-shape at the lower left, this time. Magically, the
water mountains of Jungle Island drained away, and
a moment later, new mountains of different shapes
arose from the L-shaped plateau below me and to my left. There could be no
doubt, now that I was looking down upon an elaborate and astonishingly
complex kind of topographical map.

I experimented some more, searching now for what I knew must be there.
Four of the islands were obviously the three I already knew, plus the new one
I was now on. Jungle Island, as noted, was at the lower right, the largest of the
five. Temple Island, my starting point, was immediately above—to the north.
Crater Island, the large square with its central lake, was at the upper left, while
the L-shaped Plateau Island at lower left was clearly the site of my current
explorations.

The fifth island remained a mystery. Isolated and alone, off to the northwest
of the others, it alone did not seem to have a counterpart within the real
world. Looking beyond the boundaries of the island, I could clearly see Jungle
Island, the real Jungle Island, in the distance; but I could detect no sign of the
small island on the horizon beyond and to the right. If it existed—and I knew
that it must—it must be far removed indeed from these others.

I now knew something else, as well, another small and potentially useful piece
of information. The squared-off shapes on the brass plaque were shapes that
I had seen and sketched before. I'd seen them in the Gate Room, drawn on
stained glass in the illuminated displays within the golden beetles. I'd seen them
again, later, on that plaque on the railing inside the Great Golden Dome. There,
I'd speculated that they represented buildings of some kind, but I knew now
that my speculations had been erroneous. Those collections of small squares
arranged in different, interlocking shapes represented not buildings but islands.

And most recently I had seen those shapes in Gehn's journal.

The Golden Dome provided power, I thought, via those immense pipes I'd seen within its cavernous interior, power transmitted to each of Riven's five islands.

Power, I wondered, for what? Most of each island's needs seemed to be provided by on-site geothermal power—the bollard in the center of the lake on Crater Island, for instance, with the valve feeding power to the log chipper, the boiler, or the frog-catching facility in turn. Perhaps there was some mechanism I did not as yet recognize that required energy in sudden and unusually large amounts.

I elected to leave the plateau maps as I'd found them, pressing the last key I'd pressed a second time to drain the water away and return the entire display to its initial state. There appeared to be nothing more to be learned here, and a further exploration of this island's interior seemed in order.

I had but a single path open to me, back the way I'd come, through the elevator and beyond through the cleft in the rock. I emerged at yet another central, crater lake and a structure as strange as any I'd yet encountered in my journeys here.

It was round and squat, forged from metal gone rusty and adrift in the water on a whitish doughnut of a float. D'ni script cut from metal decorated the base of the object, and I could just glimpse dark mysteries within through the spaces afforded by the decorative letters. The structure appeared anchored and motionless, but there was no walkway, no gangplank or bridge that I could see that would allow me to approach it. Baffled for the moment, I elected to explore elsewhere.

I looked up. The immense blade of a titanic knife extended from the crevice in the rock above and behind me, its pointed end nearly touching the structure. This, I realized, was the other end of the enormous knife hilt I'd seen above the overlook on the other side. What was the significance of the knives? Who had written them into this Age, and why?

A wood-planked catwalk branched left and right ahead of me, just short of the floating, round building. To my left, far around the curve of the lake, I

could just make out another of those spinning marble domes, visible behind a sharp, V-shaped cleft in the rock crater wall. Walking around the sweep of the lake, I took a closer look. The dome appeared to be identical to the ones I'd seen previously on Temple and Crater Islands and—although I'd seen it only from an unreachable distance from the base of its strange, stone pillar—on Jungle Island as well. The now-familiar symbols engraved within the spinning dome's side appeared the same as the others. I strained my eyes, trying to identify the one picked out in yellow that would be the key to stopping its rotation and was pretty sure I could distinguish it as it flashed around: a circle with a horizontal line through the middle. That should be easy enough to capture within the kinetoscope once I found it. I couldn't see the unlocking mechanism nearby, however; I decided to do some more exploring around the sides of the lake.

While at this vantage point, though, I decided to study the round building more closely. I could learn nothing from the exterior; the only door seemed to be directly opposite the cleft from which I'd emerged, just beneath the projecting knife blade, and there was nothing anywhere on or near the water like a bridge. Four curious structures caught my eye, however, wooden idols—or perhaps totems was the better word—rising from the dark waters of the lake. Yet again, it seemed, the monstrous wahrk was represented, here in wood crudely shaped and garishly painted. Each totem possessed a different color scheme picked out within the stripes painted on its arched back, this one blue, that one orange, then yellow, then green.

Continuing my tradition of claiming explorer's prerogative and naming my finds, I decided to call this place Totem Lake.

I found the kinetoscope on the far side of the lake, mounted on a platform that looked across the lake, past the floating building, and into the cleft with its turning dome. This would not be an easy one to use, however, for someone—the vandalism was clearly deliberate—had smashed the side of the kinetoscope, knocking the delicately aligned instrument far to the left and twisting it out of line. I couldn't see how to fix the thing. Defeated, I returned to the cleft by the elevator.

I was stymied now, with no place else to go. No bridge to the floating building, which clearly was of some considerable importance here. No way to stop the spinning dome. Nothing more to be learned at the overlook.

Or was there? Returning through the elevator, I walked up to the brass plate and pressed the L-shaped key representing the island I was currently investigating, the one I was thinking of as Plateau Island. I was beginning to formulate a theory.

Returning through the cleft, I emerged on the catwalk and was delighted to find that my theory, my guess, really, had been accurate. A walkway now extended from the intersection of the catwalks, reaching across the water to the open door of the floating, spherical building.

The purpose of the last island I'd explored, clearly, was book making. The purpose of this island, I'd decided, had to do more with maps than with books, with its aerial view of Riven's islands, and a device that rendered the terrain visible in watery, three-dimensional detail.

If my conjecture was true, the spherical building dealt with map making as well and was connected somehow to the island plateaus. More answers, I thought, would be forthcoming inside.

And I was right.

The floating structure proved to house a single large, circular room and appeared constructed for the sole purpose of sheltering an immense dais at its precise center. Climbing the short flight of steps that led to the top, I wasn't quite prepared for what I would find.

It was a mapping facility of some kind, and very clearly connected in some way with the plateau islands outside. A large tank, fully six feet across, occupied the center of the building; inside the tank was a square apparently composed of tens of thousands of tiny metal studs gleaming in the light filtering through the open script, decorations from the water outside. The square was divided into a five-by-five grid—that number, again!—by red lines painted on the metal studs.

In front of me, within easy reach, a graphic representation of the L-shaped island lay within a circled disk with a single handle at the side, resembling nothing so much as a large magnifying glass. The topmost of the Plateau Island's four smaller squares was illuminated somehow from within. Cautiously, I touched the illuminated square.

Instantly, with a greasy squeak of metal, the thousands of studs comprising the surface of the large square in the tank rose before me. Have you ever seen one of those museum exhibits or curiosities composed of a frame within which hundreds of pins dangle side by side? Reach your hand beneath the frame and bring it up against the hanging points of the pins; the pinheads rise at your touch to form an eerie, three-dimensional relief of your outstretched palm and fingers. This was like that, although it was not my hand raising the three-dimensional relief, but something else, an agency unseen beneath the tank which was representing in faithful detail what I thought must be the terrain within the small, illuminated square representing the island.

The detail of this topological study was much sharper than that revealed by the water mountains outside. I touched the handle on the magnifying glass, and the graphic image inside ratcheted about counterclockwise by ninety degrees; the larger relief display in the tank turned as well, showing the same changed aspect, permitting a closer and more detailed examination. Touching another of the squares erased the first map and replaced it with another, this one, I assumed, of the new square. I soon found, with a bit of experimentation, that I could actually recognize some features. The native forms, the mountains, the canyons, the silhouettes of the mountains, all were rendered in distinct and easily recognized form on the map. One of the squares clearly showed the monoliths, while another depicted the five island plateaus and the cleft running between them. Totem Lake was easy to recognize, though neither the map building nor the wahrk totems were visible.

This facility, I decided, had been designed as a survey station of some kind, a means of studying and mapping all of the scattered isles of Riven.

How to view the other islands? That seemed obvious, if a bit laborious and repetitious. Leaving the building, walking back down the catwalk, through the tunnel and the elevator and out onto the overlook, I touched another of the island symbols on the brass plate. This time it was the one representing, as I thought, Crater Island. Retracing my steps again, I reached the survey building and its raised, central dais to find that my surmise had been correct once more. The map graphic of Crater Island, a large square divided into four square quadrants, was there for my inspection.

Here, too, the geological features I remembered from my explorations there were revealed to my analytical gaze. I could even see the hole or gap in the top of a mountain that, I knew, lay directly above the hidden chamber where Crater Island's Fire Marble Dome was sequestered.

Having learned how the mapping facility worked, I was left with an even greater mystery: What was it all for? There had to be some common factor, but what could it be? Jungle Island, Crater Island, and Plateau Island all possessed crater lakes ringed by mountain walls, but that was not true of Temple Island—unless you counted the boiling pool with the golden dome itself— nor did it seem to be true of the unexplored and mysterious fifth island. What was that common factor?

And then I saw, I thought, the connection. It struck me in stages, one blow at a time, as piece by piece the mystery fell into place. Where had I seen a grid before, like this one in front of me? The dark gray plate with its twenty-five by twenty-five array of holes, clearly, in the upper level of the Great Golden Dome. Six colored marbles had rested in niches to one side, and the holes in the grid seemed designed to receive those marbles, no doubt in a particular pattern representing some code that would trigger whatever it was that the Golden Dome was supposed to do.

And what might that pattern be? A chill tingled its way up my spine and across the base of my head. What was the one feature common to every island I'd visited thus far?

The Fire Marble Domes. Of *course*!

With a new and burning sense of urgency, I began studying the relief maps anew. The red grids divided each of the smaller island squares into twenty- five squares; all of the islands together could be combined like the pieces of a jigsaw puzzle, forming a single square divided into… yes! Twenty-five squares. Twenty-five times twenty-five is six hundred twenty-five, the same number as the number of holes in the marble grid in the giant dome.

I was now willing to bet everything, even the possibility of my returning home, that the key to the Golden Dome puzzle lay *here*, in the map room. What I needed was to find some means of recording the location of each Fire Marble Dome in Riven, using the squares and red-lined grid as a coor- dinate system. I pulled out my notebook and began writing feverishly, paus- ing only to make additional trips to the overlook to change the map settings to a different island, or to manipulate the map room controls for a different vantage point.

Once I knew what I was looking for, the domes were not difficult to find. I couldn't actually see the dome on Crater Island, but I had already identified its location. This island's dome was visible on one of the two squares showing Totem Lake. Temple Island and Jungle Island were much larger than the others, with five and eleven squares respectively, but I needn't search all the squares. I was reasonably certain of the relative locations of the domes, and in fact they proved quite easy to spot.

As for the fifth island, well, it must have a Fire Marble Dome as well. I remembered the plaque inside the entrance to the giant dome which had shown the graphic symbols for the five islands and showed each connected to the golden dome by a massive pipe. Those pipes, I thought now, powered the domes or, rather, powered what was *inside* them.

Linking books!

The question was, where was the dome on the fifth island? I'd not been there; I couldn't even *see* the place from any of the four islands I'd visited. I ventured to the relief map as my guide. Fortunately, the fifth island was claustrophobically small. It looked small and round, with a broad, flat top; I doubted that the dome was there, however, for there was no place else on that speck of rock where habitation or large buildings could be raised. However, to my delight, I noted, a circular patch of flat-topped rock next to the island proper, and I tentatively assigned that as the fifth island's marble dome location.

The pieces were coming together very well indeed. I now knew, I thought, what the marble grid in the Great Golden Dome was for, and how it was used. One remaining piece of the puzzle remained, however. In the golden dome's upper level, there'd been *six* colored marbles. That meant I would have to choose five of the six; I remembered having read something in Gehn's lab journal about how the D'ni had used a six-color symbology, but that he, Gehn, had been convinced that a greater symbology lay within the use of five colors only.

That number, yet again!

Clearly it mattered what color went in which place, but I had no clue, as yet, to what color was assigned to which island. I tried to think about where I had seen colors and under what circumstances. The golden dome… no, that was the same as the fire marble dome colors. Then I had it. The wahrk totems, in the lake right outside! There had been four, each painted with colored stripes—blue, orange, yellow, and green. I thought, now, that I knew at least four of the colors I would need to solve the puzzle.

But how could I learn which color went with which island?

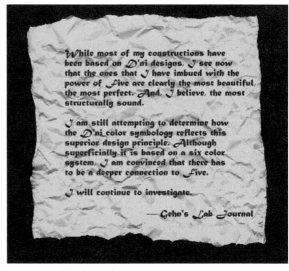

While most of my constructions have been based on D'ni designs, I see now that the ones that I have imbued with the power of Five are clearly the most beautiful, the most perfect. And, I believe, the most structurally sound.

I am still attempting to determine how the D'ni color symbology reflects this superior design principle. Although superficially it is based on a six color system, I am convinced that there has to be a deeper connection to Five.

I will continue to investigate.

—Gehn's Lab Journal

There seemed to be nothing else to be learned here. I was certain, though, that I'd not yet exhausted the mysteries of Plateau Island. There was that orange-lit subterranean pool I'd glimpsed in my trek here from the tram. There was also the matter of that inaccessible door I'd seen at the tram station. If I could gain access to that door, more possibilities might become available.

I thought about that other door as I rode the elevator back down to the plateau below, then again as I followed the jagged, crack-like line of the walkway through the pool and among the towering plateau island maps. I'd seen no other doors in my investigation of this island thus far; the secret had to be at the tram station below.

And by the time I reached the tram once more, I knew what the answer was.

Whistling a light and jaunty air, I stepped back up into the waiting tram and took my seat, then turned the control lever that rotated the car, swinging about until the vehicle's prow aimed once again at the glistening sea.

I rose and stepped out.

It was that simple, and I was feeling inordinately smug as I opened the mysterious door glimpsed earlier and entered an eerie, orange-lit passageway. Riven was a place where the obvious was sometimes less than obvious, where one was forced to assume a particularly devious twist of mind in order to perform the simplest acts.

The passageway ended before long in an underground pool within a great, black pentagon, and I recognized at once that I was at the subterranean spot I'd seen earlier, on the path among the monoliths. A lever with yellow stripes rose from the walkway at the left. Since the way appeared to be a dead end at the pool, I pulled the lever. In moments, massive chains to either side of the path sank down, and the water before me swirled, then broke as a golden box emerged, still turning from the depths. It rose until it rested atop the water's surface, and then a door like a narrow drawbridge opened, lowering a walkway to my feet.

Nonplused by this peculiar invitation, I crossed the walkway and entered what was clearly another elevator cage; inside, I pressed the button. The door closed, sealing tightly, and in another moment I was descending beneath the waves.

I'm honestly not certain about what happened next, for I was clearly under-water and yet, when the cage stopped its descent and rotation and the door creaked open once more, it deposited me within a chamber, sealed off from the water. A tunnel mouth provided my only egress from the cave, and I fol-lowed it, my sense of direction now thoroughly scrambled by dark and repeated turnings.

I walked for a long way—as long, I thought, counting off my steps, as it had taken for me to reach the island plateaus on the surface, and the two-way elevator beyond. Movement ahead at the end of the tunnel caught my eye. A man! He saw me at the same instant and seemed at least as startled by the encounter as I was. As I moved forward, he darted through an opening in the left side of the passageway, vanishing into a side room. Moments later, panti-ng with exertion, I pounded into the room after him just in time to see him at the controls of another of the trams, which was already pivoting about in place, then drifting forward through a gap in the stone wall above the open sea. Riding effortlessly, frictionlessly on invisible and silent cushions of mag-netic force, the tram glided into daylight and swiftly shot across the ocean in the direction of Jungle Island.

I doubted that the man I'd just seen was Gehn himself. The white robes he'd affected suggested that he might have been a scribe or acolyte, a member of the religious order centering around the worship of Gehn.

Well, no matter. Gehn certainly knew already that I was here. Any warning the fleeing man could spread would carry no more information than what was obvious. I was *here*.

I left the tram chamber, although I made a mental note to come back this way on my way out. When I concluded with Plateau Island, taking a tram back to Jungle Island—and to an unexplored portion of Jungle Island, at that—would be preferable to retracing my steps all the way across Crater Island, then by that unsettling log car ride back to Jungle Island.

Back in the long passageway, I turned left and kept going, emerging at last in a cavernous room with an enormous glass window looking out into the depths of an aquatic world. I climbed a long straight stairway to reach a kind of elevated throne, then touched a button that rotated the throne into place. *Gehn's Aquarium* was the thought that came first to mind, although I doubted, somehow, that he was all that interested in sea life, except, possibly, for the wahrks. Certainly, though, this was an observation chamber of some sort.

Two handles or levers presented themselves to me, one on the left, the other on the right. Reaching out, I grasped the right lever and pulled it down. A circular device, cast in heavy metal, lowered itself from my right, positioning itself just in front of me.

It was a curious design. At the center was a screen of some kind, while the face of the device bore six pentagonal buttons in a circle about the screen. There were also six tabs with finger holes extending in a circle about the thing's body, clearly designed for ease of turning. A kind of wire loop at the bottom framed one of the buttons.

I felt a sudden thrill of recognition. Each button bore a symbol, and many of those symbols I knew! There was the circle with the central dot, which had opened the Fire Marble Dome on Temple Island. There was the circle with the vertical line that, I was sure, opened the dome here on Plateau Island. There was the circle with the horizontal line that had opened the subterranean dome on Crater Island.

Using the tabs, I turned the outer wheel, rotating the buttons through the wire frame, until the circle with the dot was captured. So far so good; the button bearing that symbol depressed easily beneath my thumb, and, in the central screen, a green light winked on. Excited, now, I began experimenting. Each symbol, it seemed, represented a color and I could scarcely contain the pounding of my heart in my chest as I realized that here, right before me, was the missing piece of the marble-grid puzzle. The marble representing the Temple Island Fire Marble Dome would be *green*. I knew it! Plateau Island's symbol stood for orange. One by one, I tested each symbol, noting the color.

One, the symbol for Crater Island, elicited no response, and I finally decided that it must be broken. The more I thought about what I was seeing, the more sure I was that this observation chamber looked out into the lake upon which the Map Chamber floated. It might, in fact, be directly over my head! The colored lights I could see in the screen, I decided, must be affixed under water to the bases of those painted wahrk totems I'd seen. There'd been four, which in a world that seemed mesmerized by the number five suggested that there was a missing totem on the lake. I would have to guess at what that color might have been.

I recorded the other symbols and colors, however. I still hadn't seen the symbol at the Jungle Island Fire Marble Dome, of course, so I didn't know whether it would be blue, red, or yellow. The fifth island, too, was an unknown and might be any of those colors. I had two identified, however, and that was a very respectable start.

I happened to have the red light on when, for some reason, I chanced to glance up from the tiny screen at my lap… and nearly died of heart failure! The red light was there, glowing in the dark water a few feet from the glass wall encircling me.

And there was also a wahrk!

I couldn't move, couldn't even breathe, as I stared at that titanic, that spectacular apparition. It was aware of me, I knew; it turned its head slightly and regarded me through a tiny, knowing eye. It skin was supple, with scattering of warts or bumps; its tail, not at all like that of a fish, was rather the horizontal flukes of a whale. Overall, the thing must have been thirty feet in length, whale-like, indeed, with tusks like those of an elephant projecting from its massive, lower jaw. I could hear through the glass its call, a low, eerie, lost-soul moan something like the dirge of a humpback whale, the same sound, in fact, that I'd heard so long ago on Jungle Island, when I turned the wooden eye affixed to the wahrk-shaped rock.

And then, as silent as a wraith, the monster was gone, vanished into the dark shadows of the lake. Had it been summoned by the light? Perhaps it associated that signal with food. No matter. I had what I needed now from the Color Wheel, and I was not about to experiment with Gehn's huge and dangerous pets!

I did want to learn what the other lever did, however. Raising the Color Wheel, I next pulled down the lever to my left and was rewarded when a similar device dropped from my left, almost into my lap. This one was simpler than the other. It bore but two buttons, one on either side of the same sort of small, round screen, and six tabs bearing finger holes. I touched the left-side button, and was rewarded by a small, distorted view of what looked like a woman, pacing alone in a room somewhere.

The image shocked me nearly as much as had the sight of the wahrk. Was this some kind of spy device? A way to peep into someone's home? On the screen, the woman rose and walked toward an opening into daylight just visible beyond; I thought I could catch a glimpse there of the sea, and an iron railing. She was dark-haired and very beautiful, moving with a sad and dignified grace.

Catherine. The woman *had* to be Catherine! I thought now that I must be looking into her prison. Where might it be? Somewhere else here on Plateau Island, perhaps? Possibly the mysterious fifth island? There were no clues in the small and blurry image transmitted to the spy-screen. I pushed the right-side button.

The first scene I saw was dark and difficult to make out, but as I used the finger tabs to rotate the device, other scenes came into view, one of which I immediately recognized. It was a low-angle view of the docks below the native village on Jungle Island. Thinking back, I remembered the device like a telescope or camera lens extending from a small, low rock rising above the surface of Village Lake. This room, then, was where the images captured were relayed and viewed. I pulled at one of the finger tabs and the device rotated, bringing another view from the lake to the screen. There were six such scenes, I learned, looking in different directions across the lake. There was the wahrk gallows. Three of them were too dark to make out much detail, but in addition to the village dock I could see an upper catwalk casting shadows on the cliff wall and also the base of the wahrk gallows with its supporting cables reflected in the still waters of the lake. I ran through the series once more to see if I could detect anything more of interest.

Odd. I leaned closer, trying to get a better view of the image of the catwalk. *Very* odd! From this angle, a low-ceilinged cavern in the side of the rock wall beside the lake, and the mirror-inverted reflection in the water beneath, seemed to form a startling dark silhouette; the outline of a fish with triangular fins. And there, about where the fish's eye should be, there was something I couldn't quite make out. Yes! A wooden Eye, attached somehow to the rock of the cavern just above the water!

Quite serendipitously, I had discovered the fifth animal silhouette, the one I had associated with the Eye I had seen in Gehn's lab!

By the time I left Gehn's Survey Room, I had a great deal to think about. I now knew two of the five colors I needed identified, and I knew what other symbols to look for. I'd also found the missing piece of another puzzle, one that I'd put away for a time since I'd left Jungle Island. I now had a list of five animals, identified either by sound or by their silhouette, and with each there was an associated numeral, one through five. I was certain that the solution to this puzzle would lead me to the Moiety…and perhaps Catherine. All I needed now was to learn just where that particular puzzle solution should be applied!

I had no doubt that I would find out sooner or later.

I made my way down the steps, then out and to the right, into the chamber where I'd seen the white-robed figure make his escape. I boarded the tram when it arrived, rotated it, and moved the start lever forward.

I was actually beginning to get used to these things, I thought. It helped a lot if I closed my eyes.

The tram station led me directly into a wooden elevator. Lifting the lever to my right, I ascended a considerable distance straight up, not rotating this time, and stopped facing a blue tram call button and a set of descending stairs apparently leading nowhere. I took a cautious step forward and noticed a lever on the wall to my left. When I pressed it, the floor in front of me creaked open, like a hinged trap door with jagged teeth. Another step or two enabled me to recognize my surroundings. I had emerged from *inside* the giant Wahrk Idol in the Jungle! Well, that was one mystery solved, but I still needed a means of accessing the Fire Marble Dome. It was most disconcerting. I could *see* the thing spinning above me, I could *see* the catwalks criss-crossing the jungle canopy, but what I *couldn't* see was a way up.

I walked around outside the idol for a bit, looking carefully for anything that might provide a hint of a direction in which to go. On the tree above the Wahrk Idol I noticed what might have been a doorway, but it wasn't directly above the idol. Even if the elevator went up another level, that wouldn't help, unless… unless it rotated, like the golden elevator back on Plateau Island! It was certainly worth a try.

I raced back inside the idol, closed the mouth again, and raised the lever. Yes! The chamber rotated counterclockwise about 60 degrees and then rose to the level of the catwalk. A step or two forward assured me that I was on the level of the dome. As I approached the dome, I noticed a catwalk exiting to the right of the main catwalk. I bypassed the side path for the moment but noted it for future reference. Face to face with the spinning dome, I could almost make out the yellow symbol. It looked as though two arcs cutting across the middle of the circle were forming a rough eye shape, but I couldn't mark it down with any degree of certainty, as I had done for the dome on Plateau Island.

As I walked around the side of the dome, still searching for the kinetoscope I knew must be here, I noticed a stairway going up. It appeared to lead to the catwalk I had observed above me when I first exited the Jungle. Sure enough, as I climbed, I saw, poking up above the foliage that rimmed the jungle, the guard tower that had sounded the alert before and heard a repetition of its mournful wail.

Crossing the catwalk, I found myself facing a small round tower flanked by stone monoliths. The door easily opened to reveal a throne surmounted by what looked to be the lower jawbone, complete with tusks, of a wahrk. In fact, the room consisted of nothing but the throne. I sat down with a shudder of distaste and manipulated the levers I saw in front of me. The right-hand one was immobile, but when I pulled back on the left-hand lever, the tower roof rolled back out of the way and the throne rose up, rotating counterclockwise as it did so to present me with a spectacular view of the Cliff Village overlooking Village Lake. I looked around to orient myself and found that I was directly above the Wahrk Gallows. This must be the vantage point from which Gehn observed his victims being callously fed to the wahrks.

A plank led from the top of the gallows to a walkway along the cliff wall, heading toward a circular doorway set into the cliff. What better place to keep prisoners prior to their execution! I wished I could ride the gallows bar up to that walkway and investigate . . . but I had been unable to reach the bar from the base of the gallows.

On a whim, I tried the right-hand lever again to find that it was no longer inactive. Pushing it forward caused five panels to rotate underneath the gallows walkway, forming a closed platform marked with Gehn's seal. Perhaps now I would be able to ride the bar up to the level of the upper catwalk and investigate what I felt sure was Gehn's prison.

But first I needed to find that kinetoscope. A push on the left-hand lever returned the throne to its former place, and I returned to the canopy pathways in the Jungle. My only hope remaining was the catwalk that went off to the side. That catwalk went out and around and ended directly opposite the dome, unveiling the missing kinetoscope! It was a simple matter to catch the eye-shaped symbol in the lens and open the dome.

The locking device appeared to be the same as on the other two domes I had opened. The time had obviously come for me to figure out that code I had found in Gehn's journal and discover if it worked as I expected. I sat down with my journal and wrote out on a new sheet the series of numbers I had found and, next to it, the numerals 1 through 10. It seemed to be, at least on some level, a numeric system based on five. All the numbers consisted of squares with additional marks inside them. The first five symbols were fairly simple, having no lines crossing inside the squares. The next four, however, looked as though they might have been formed from a combination of symbols. All of the numbers from six to nine consisted of the horizontal line that represented five, plus some other line or combination of lines. Six, for example, had a horizontal and a vertical line crossing in the middle, a combination of five and one. Seven had the same horizontal line for the number five, but over top of it the curved line that represented the number two. Ten, however, was different. It consisted, like the number two, of a single curved line running from one corner of the square to the adjacent corner, but two ran from top left to bottom left, whereas 10 ran from bottom left to bottom right.

In other words, 10 was two rotated 90 degrees counterclockwise. Was that the pattern I was looking for? Six through nine were built by adding on to five. Would 11 through 14 be built the same way, by adding on to 10? Of course! Five was nothing more than one rotated 90 degrees. So if five was a rotated one and 10 was a rotated two, then 15 must be a rotated three and 20 a rotated four! Adding one to four to those base numbers yielded the rest of the numbers. Quickly I jotted down the numbers in rows of five. It worked! I had all the numbers from one to 24!

Now the code I'd copied from Gehn's journal was making sense. Reading from left to right, the numbers were 3, 8, 11, 16, 22. I wondered how this system handled the numbers beyond twenty-five, or for that matter, the number twenty-five itself. Rotating five would simply yield another one. There must be a different symbol for twenty-five.

Now was the time to test my deductions. I approached the locking device inside the Fire Marble Dome. I had five numbers in the code, and there were five sliders on the lock. The bar was divided into five groups of five, for a total of twenty-five, and I had 24 digits I was sure of. I moved the rightmost slider over to position 22 and placed the other sliders accordingly. Then I pressed the button. The sliders clicked back to their original position and nothing happened for about three seconds. Then the golden dome rotated away and the outer dome rotated back, leaving me inside facing a Linking Book as it rose up on a stand out of the base of the dome.

Cautiously I approached the Book and noticed two numbers on the outside cover, a nine followed by an eight. Another code? Or did this pair of numbers somehow identify the destination of this Book? That particular juxtaposition of digits looked familiar to me. I leafed through the notes I had been keeping in Artrus's journal. Yes, there it was! That was the number of Gehn's Age, the Age to which his journal

indicated that these domes were designed to provide a means of transport. There was no doubt about it. I had found a way to reach Gehn.

But was I ready to meet him yet?

Did I have a choice?

I opened the Book and discovered that my fears were moot—the Book was not powered. Powering the Books was a task I still had to undertake. Perhaps the Marble Grid inside the Great Golden Dome was involved somehow, as I'd speculated earlier.

But I had not yet completed my investigations of this island. I was certain I had identified Gehn's prison above the ominously waiting Wahrk Gallows. Suppose Catherine were there? No, I had to continue my search for Catherine before I attempted to trap Gehn.

As I was walking back to the elevator, I pondered the meaning of the numeric notation on the outside of the Linking Book. Surely "98" didn't mean the same thing I was accustomed to. Perhaps a positional notation, like my own, but based on twenty-five rather than on ten? I quickly performed the calculation— nine times twenty-five and add eight—and stared hard at the result…233. Could that be right? Had Gehn written and discarded so many Ages as that?

Shaking my head in disbelief, I emerged on the floor of the Jungle through the gaping mouth of the Wahrk Idol. As I walked between the two lamps that flanked the path, I noticed that one of them had a knob extending up from the base. I was certain I hadn't remembered that from my first foray into the Jungle, so I pressed it. As I suspected, the mouth of the idol closed. I pulled it and the mouth opened. I could have gotten to the Fire Marble Dome at any time if only I noticed that knob!

On the other hand, I wouldn't have recognized the Wahrk Gallows for what it was when viewing it from Gehn's Throne if I hadn't already investigated the Village. I needed to explore all the islands in any case. Did the order in which I accomplished that really matter?

I closed the idol's mouth and continued on my way. As I approached the giant stone pillar that was the base of the Fire Marble Dome, I was aston- ished to see a Rivenese child staring at me. She turned abruptly and ran away, stumbling and falling but then picking herself up quickly and disap- pearing into the pillar. I cursed my inability to communicate with these poor people. All of a sudden figuring out the D'ni numbering system no longer seemed such an impressive accomplishment.

Turning right after I left the Jungle, I quickly proceeded down the path to the Village, finding the submarine vehicle still parked at the Village Dock. Now that I understood the geography of this underwater transport system, it was a matter of moments to return to the base of the Wahrk Gallows. As I crossed the platform, I glanced up in the direction of Gehn's Throne. I could just imagine him sitting up there watching as some hapless victim was lowered down and then opening the floor at the last moment. Fiend!

It was with mixed emotions that I pulled the handle and rode the bar to the top of the gallows. I was almost reluctant to put my hand on that which had been the instrument of who knew how much misery. I felt considerable relief when I reached the top and walked across the plank toward the circular door in the cliff wall. The door was not solid but consisted of five sets of bars approaching the center at different angles, so I could readily see inside. Somehow I was not surprised to see a man in Rivenese dress and wearing a red band around his forehead sitting on the bare stone floor. He appeared to be asleep as he leaned against the wall, but as I approached, he raised his head, stared at me steadily for a moment, and then relapsed into slumber.

I had undoubtedly found the prison, but what could I do about it? Not a solitary thing. My impotence in this situation infuriated me. I scanned my surroundings quickly and was pleased to discover a knob on the cliff wall to my right. Not unexpectedly, it bore the five-pointed star symbol on the base and the number five on the knob itself. I pulled the knob and turned it, noting to my delight that the prison door was opening, but although I raced back to the door as quickly as I could, when I entered the cell, the prisoner was not there!

I was struck dumb. It was impossible! Where could he have gone? I had been watching the door the entire time that it was dilating, there was no other opening in the cell, nothing save a six-inch grate on the floor, nothing else in the cell at all other than a battered plate, presumably to hold a meager ration of food for the short time Gehn would permit between arrest and execution. There was *no* place he could have gone!

After a none-too-brief moment, I regained my senses, realizing that if there were no visible means of escape from this chamber, then the prisoner must have escaped by means that were no longer visible. With a calmer heart I was able to notice that some of the stones in the far wall appeared imperfectly mortared. Now all I needed was to be able to detect the key. The one obvious place to search was the grate, so I knelt down and pried it open. It flipped back on its hinge quite easily, leaving me no alternative but to stick my hand down into the pool of brown slime. Somewhat to my surprise— after all, it was truly unlikely that the obvious place would be the *correct* place—my hand soon found a handle. As I tugged it out of the water, I heard a grinding sound as of stone against metal. I looked up to see that section of wall receding on a metal track, revealing a passageway beyond.

I eagerly clambered through into the beginnings of a tunnel through the mountain. As I started down the passageway, I heard the wall close behind me. Turning, I noticed another handle similar to the one that had opened the wall for me. Somewhat assured that I would have a means of return, I began to creep along the darkening—and soon pitch black—passage. I was reminded of my journey through the water pipe on Crater Island. Although I was unable to see my hand in front of my face, at least this time I could make the traverse in an upright position!

After what felt like a frighteningly long time, but what was likely no more than a minute or two, I detected a glimmer of light in the distance. Soon I was looking out on the ocean again and feeling a blessed salt sea breeze. But to what end? What had I gained by this passage? I saw nothing in this cave that could be of use… except perhaps… yes! A light, sticking out from a wall and turning on at my touch. Now I might be able to see a bit of the return journey.

I had traveled but a short distance back when I spied yet another light globe. I lit a total of six globes in all before I found myself back at the entrance to the prison cell. I then retraced my steps, now that I could see them, searching the walls for clues I had missed in the dark. Ah, another one of those doors hiding doors! As I followed the newly revealed passageway, I marveled again at the ingenuity of these people, constructing this escape route under Gehn's very nose.

The passageway led me to a most peculiar room, an open area ringed with small upright stones, twenty-five of them, each with a different graphic symbol. They all seemed to represent animals. On the far wall a single dagger, identical in style to the one stuck in the ground on Temple Island, was framed in a niche in the stone. From my readings in the journals, I felt certain that the dagger represented the Moiety and that this chamber the means of accessing them. Now all I had to do was figure out the key.

I examined each of the symbols on the stone carefully. Some of them, certainly, I recognized. Some I had even seen on this world. I was certain that the five wooden Eyes I had discovered, each associated with a number and a particular animal and were somehow involved in this puzzle, but in what way? There were twenty-five stones and I had five animal shapes. If my five matched five of those twenty-five, then perhaps I was close to the solution. The animal silhouette on the stone directly in front of me was undoubtedly that of a wahrk. I reached out to see if the stone would be affected by my touch. Indeed, yes. With a grinding scrape it descended several inches into the floor. I touched it again and it rose to its original position.

That must be it. Touch the stones in the correct order, and, well, *something* would happen. I got out my journal to refresh my mind on the numbers and animals each Eye was associated with. Yes, the fish was one, the beetle was two, the frog—ytram, I supposed, was the correct term—was three, the sunner, four, and the wahrk, five. What a delightful irony! The rebels had been leaving their calling cards all over the island for any villager who was burning under Gehn's tyranny to see, right out in plain sight, and Gehn never realized what they were doing!

I then determined to see if my theory was correct. I found all the animal shapes and pushed them, one by one. The ytram was a bit difficult to make out—it was an extremely stylized representation—but the others were relatively easy. My heart was racing as I stood in front of the fifth and final stone. If I was right, pressing this stone would somehow open a doorway to the rebels. If I was right, I might soon be able to find Catherine. If I was wrong…

I elected not to speculate on that possibility. I pressed the stone and then stood back to see what eventuated. The result was more than I could have imagined. The entire back wall shimmered and rippled as water—performing once more in a distinctly unwatery fashion—flowed from the face of the wall to the sides and upward through channels in the rocks. The wall now glistened as though wet, and the panel on which the dagger had been displayed receded into the wall, revealing a Book. An open Book with charred edges, and over the linking area was a strange crystal window displaying a moving image of some other world. This must be the power crystal Gehn had referred to in his journal. It appeared that Catherine had managed to recover one of Gehn's failed Books and rework it to her own ends. Eager to finally meet the woman of Atrus's heart, I rested my hand on the Book and found myself overlooking a lake with high cliff walls, dwarfing those of Village Lake and Crater Lake. In the center of the lake was what looked like a giant tree stump cradling a much larger sphere with many lighted windows. Smoke arose from the center of this structure as birds with long tails and enormous wingspans swarmed around it.

I had materialized at the end of a pier, although I could see no sign of boats, either surface craft or underwater. Turning, I entered the building, a single empty chamber, empty, that is, except for the statue directly ahead of me. Garbed and deco-rated as a deity of some kind, it appeared to hold a Linking Book in its hands, with another of Catherine's power crystals resting on top of it. That, surely, would be my way back to Riven once I had completed my tasks here.

Perhaps not.

As I got close to the statue, I heard voices behind me. I turned to see the prisoner I had attempted to rescue and a rebel with a blow gun. I raised my hands in reassurance of my good intentions, but either they misread my body language or else they made a practice of blow first and ask questions later. Within a second of feeling the dart, my sight dimmed and I knew no more.

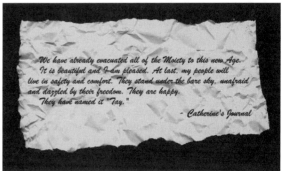

We have already evacuated all of the Moiety to this new Age. It is beautiful and I am pleased. At last, my people will live in safety and comfort. They stand under the bare sky, unafraid and dazzled by their freedom. They are happy. They have named it "Tay."

— Catherine's Journal

I regained consciousness inside a cave, with a vague memory of a watery journey and someone mumbling at me. Cautiously I got to my feet. Ahead of me, underneath the light, a large bowl sat by itself on a table. I examined my surroundings and discovered I was inside the giant globular structure in the center of the lake, and at a height that made escape impossible, even for one without such a headache as I had. In the other direction, past the table, was a dark passageway that led to a wooden gate with a window in the top. I could see large numbers of spherical buildings, miniatures, it seemed, of the giant construct in which I was a prisoner.

Although I saw several people, or at least their silhouettes, no one was close enough for me to call out to if, indeed, calling out was a choice I cared to make. I retreated silently to ponder my situation.

Coincidence, perhaps, or perhaps my spying had been noticed. In any case I had scarcely taken a dozen steps before I heard the rattle of the gate and saw a figure approach. It was a woman, dressed like a rebel but not masked, and carrying something carefully wrapped in a red cloth. She started to speak to me in an unknown tongue, but I thought her first word sounded like a form of Catherine. She unwrapped her parcel, two books, and laid them on the table, urging me most earnestly to… I knew not what. With a final beseeching look, she left me alone with her gift.

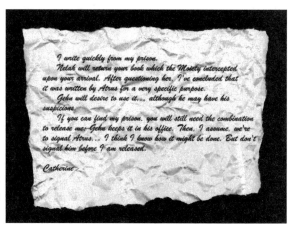

I write quickly from my prison.
Nelah will return your book which the Moiety intercepted upon your arrival. After questioning her, I've concluded that it was written by Atrus for a very specific purpose.
Gehn will desire to use it… although he may have his suspicions.
If you can find my prison, you will still need the combination to release me; Gehn keeps it in his office. Then, I assume, we're to signal Atrus… I think I know how it might be done. But don't signal him before I am released.

Catherine

Two books. The smaller I opened and saw it was a journal in a feminine hand. Could it be Catherine's? A few pages later my doubts were put to rest with a note, signed by Catherine, that had been inserted in the journal. "Nelah will return your book . . ." I quickly examined the other book. It was! It was the missing Trap Book! Now I had all I needed to complete my mission, except, of course, for such trifling matters as finding Gehn, getting him to use the Trap Book, then finding Catherine in her prison and releasing her, *then* signaling Atrus. Despite the enormity of the tasks yet facing me, though, I felt my heart lighter than it had been for some time.

Almost immediately Nelah—for it must have been her—returned with another parcel and another impassioned and unintelligible speech. Again I heard a distorted version of Catherine's name, and I longed to be able to assure her that I would indeed rescue her lady. When she departed this second time, I rejoiced to see that her present was another Linking Book with another power crystal. I could see as I approached the Book a view of the Chamber of Twenty-Five Stones that was the gateway to this world. I placed my hand on the Book and in short order was racing through the tunnel and out through the prison cell to the catwalk beyond.

My heart was hammering with excitement as I lowered a ladder to the lakeside walkway and climbed down, then skirted Village Lake on my way back to the tram station where I'd originally arrived on Jungle Island from Temple Island. Now that I had the Trap Book back in my possession, I should be able to find Gehn and see that it fell into his hands. I was reasonably certain now, thanks to my reading of the journal I'd found in Gehn's lab, that Gehn was not, in fact, on any of the isles of Riven. He'd spoken of having created a new age, where he now sought solitude and a place to conduct his experiments uninterrupted.

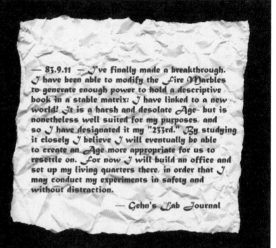

— 83.9.11 — I've finally made a breakthrough. I have been able to modify the Fire Marbles to generate enough power to hold a descriptive book in a stable matrix: I have linked to a new world! It is a harsh and desolate Age- but is nonetheless well suited for my purposes, and so I have designated it my "233rd." By studying it closely I believe I will eventually be able to create an Age more appropriate for us to resettle on. For now I will build an office and set up my living quarters there, in order that I may conduct my experiments in safety and without distraction.

— Gehn's Lab Journal

Well, I would see if I could interrupt him soon. First, though, I needed to turn on the power to the books in their various scattered Fire Marble Domes. And to do that, I would have to confront at last the Marble Puzzle in the upper level of the Great Golden Dome. I thought that now, at last, I was ready.

The tram deposited me back on Temple Island. At first, I feared a new obstacle when I saw that the door to the Temple was closed, but it opened automatically at my approach. Good. It didn't take long to make my way through the Temple, up the tunnel, across the bridge, and through the intricacies of the rotating, five-sided Gate Room. There, I approached once again the huge, dark gray square with its six hundred twenty-five holes.

Picturing the divisions of the islands, I began counting off rows and columns, carefully consulting my notebook for the coordinates I'd copied from Plateau Island. Temple Island—green, placed *there*. Jungle Island—I now knew that would be a red marble, placed *here*. Plateau Island—another easy one, *there*, at the edge of the Totem Lake.

Now the decisions got difficult. Which color was represented by a circle with a vertical line? That light had been broken on the Color Wheel, but the one color of the six left over without a matching symbol was purple. I placed that in the proper spot on Crater Island, where I'd noted the opening in the mountaintop on the map.

And that left the fifth island, an island which I was increasingly convinced must be the place where Gehn was holding Catherine captive. I had used purple, green, orange, and red. The remaining color might be yellow, or it might be blue— but which one?

I placed the yellow marble in the proper place, then walked back down the narrow corridor a way until I came to the switch on the wall. Taking a deep breath, I lowered the switch. With a rumble and a deep-throated hum, a metal plate was lowered across the neatly placed results of my labors; when the plate was in place, I reached over and thumbed a white button that had appeared above the switch.

Nothing happened.

I frowned. Was something *supposed* to happen? A blinking light? The sound of humming power? An angry guard demanding what I was doing here, in what was surely an unauthorized space?

There was no sign that anything had happened, which might mean that something about my placement of the marbles, their colors or their locations, was wrong…or it might simply mean that the mechanism was malfunctioning. Unwilling to believe that, I raised the switch again and returned to the marble grid.

Returning the yellow marble to its assigned slot, I tried the blue marble for the fifth island. If I still got no response this time, I would have to start rechecking the positions of the marbles and perhaps even begin questioning my line of reasoning. I returned to the switch and tried it again.

This time, I heard a deep, rushing whoosh, and a hot wind swirled up from the vast chamber below, howling past the metal grid and setting cables and tubes to trembling in the blast. After a few seconds, things quieted down but I felt an exultant rejoicing within, a certainty that *that* was the effect I'd been looking for.

But there was only one way to find out.

Retracing my steps, I returned to the Gate Room, then turned it until the fourth gateway was open, instead of the third. This gave me access to the catwalk leading back around and into the Golden Dome at the lower level, and I could now follow the walkway through and down and out, arriving at last at the elevator that took me down yet again, this time to the passageway leading to Temple Island's Fire Marble Dome.

I had all the pieces now. I stopped the dome with the kinetoscope, then approached the open shell and moved the sliders to the proper spots. I pushed the button and the inner seal slid open, granting me access to the waiting Link Book, embossed, as was the one on Jungle Island, with the D'ni notation for "233."

When I opened the cover and looked at the dark rectangle on the first page, I saw not blackness as I had on Jungle Island, but a moving image, an animated bird's-eye view of a strange and alien world.

What kind of place was this, I wondered? The sky was harsh, and a lake appeared to be filled with… were they trees, of some sort, like pyramids atop narrow trunks? No, they had more the look of stone about them, but what weirdly twisted geology could produce such bizarre shapes from native rock? One rock had a structure atop it, obviously artificial. This, I presumed, was Gehn's fortress of solitude, his world away from the world of Riven. With trembling hand, I touched the image…

…and found myself behind bars again!

Well, that was to be expected, of course; Gehn must dread having the odd rebel or Atrus himself figure out the puzzles and drop by unannounced. The cell was large enough for standing, but little else. The room I was imprisoned in possessed broad, glass walls looking out into that alien world. Benches held various items and papers, and a feeling of busyness and clutter.

Of particular interest were five Link Books arrayed about the perimeter of my cell, beyond the bars but within easy reach, each at the focus of a device of some sort evidently designed to feed them power. Each was embossed with the number five and the symbol of a different Rivenese island; I opened the one bearing the single, small square that I now was certain represented Catherine's Prison Island, but the picture inside was black and lifeless. These books, it seemed, needed to be powered, just as had the Link Book that had brought me here.

Still, I realized that *this* was how to reach Catherine's island, the only route I had seen so far on any of my travels.

There was also, I noticed, a square affixed to the inside of my cage with a single button at the center of an engraving of Gehn's star symbol. Well, it might open the cage or it might summon Gehn or a guard. Either way, it was worth a try. I pressed the button.

Nothing happened at first, other than the illuminating of the star, but after a moment I saw a figure approaching the building from outside, an old man, I thought, but still hard and strong and powerful, a regal individual. When I saw his face, I saw that this was indeed the man I'd glimpsed in the holographic imaging cage in the School Room.

He wore a heavy white coat similar to, if richer than, the garb worn by the guard I'd first encountered. He wore heavy goggles of some sort over his eyes; they looked a bit ludicrous, even out of place but I decided that the harsh light of this world's sun must present a threat to unprotected eyes. He also wore heavy gloves, which confirmed that conditions here must be somewhat hostile, and he carried a cane with an elaborate head, the twin of the one I'd noticed on a workbench back in his lab or even, perhaps, the same one.

He spent a great deal of time trying to convince me that he was not the man he once was.

I had to admit that Gehn actually was a pleasant sort, and the reason and rationality behind his words did tug at me as I listened. Thirty years he'd been a prisoner on Riven. "Thirty years," he declaimed, "thirty lifetimes! What does it matter?" Nothing could atone, he claimed, for what he'd once been. Yes, he'd imprisoned Catherine—he specifically asked me not to try to free her—since he'd been forced to keep her apart from her rebels, to whom she'd become a kind of savior, a messianic figure.

But in these past days, I'd come to know Gehn, the *real* Gehn, very well, I thought. If the natives thought Catherine to be their savior, Gehn had gone out of his way to convince them of his godhood. He'd cultivated those great, majestic sea beasts as pets, as prey and as executioners for his bloody spectacles. Oh, I had no doubt that he would defend his actions on the grounds of the needs, the *higher* needs of all society, but the Wahrk Gallows and the grim lesson of the wooden toy in the School Room suggested that he used the executions less for the good of society than to maintain his personal power.

He trapped those beautiful, jewel-like frogs for an extract which he then smoked. As I watched him prepare a strangely shaped pipe while he talked and puff it alight, I felt sick to my stomach. Gehn had *not* changed, whatever the honey on his words. For him, Riven, the people of Riven, the trees, the wahrks, the frogs, Catherine, and I myself were all tools to be *used* with neither emotion nor consideration, tools to apply to his immediate need or whim, and then to be discarded.

I could tell he wanted desperately to try the Trap Book. He took it from me and hovered above the image, the moving picture promising him the freedom and knowledge of lost D'ni. His face took on the predatory look of some great bird of prey, his hand like a grasping claw, his eyes alight with eagerness at the phantom promise. *Touch it! Touch it!* I thought, willing him to lay hand upon image and so fall into the trap.

And then, the fire in his eyes was replaced by a colder, a deeper cunning, and his hand pulled back. "Perhaps," he said, "it would be best if you went through first!" He held the book up for my touch.

It was, of course, a test. If I refused, he would become suspicious of this gift, a Link Book, apparently, promising him everything he wanted—freedom, access to the secrets of D'ni, access, indeed, to all the worlds of the cosmos. And, of course, if I went through, I would be trapped instead of Gehn.

Before I could formulate a reply, before I could even think, he withdrew the offered page. "You may need some time to decide," he told me. Placing the book on a desk, he walked over to a large, round construction nearby and moved a switch, eliciting a full-voiced roar, as from a furnace. Power flickered across the devices focused on the Linking Books near my cage. "Until then," he continued, "I will allow you free access to my Linking Books and the rest of the Fifth Age. Please don't signal me unless you've decided to use the book."

Donning gloves and goggles once more, he stepped into the harsh, ultraviolet-laden light of his 233rd world's sun and disappeared.

I did not hesitate. I *could* not. By extraordinary good fortune, Gehn had left me the means I'd sought to reach Catherine's island. Without hesitation, I moved to that book, opened the cover, and laid my hand upon the image that now appeared on the page.

Catherine's Island, as I now thought of the place, was a lonely, forsaken rock embraced by the roots and lower trunk of what once had been a titanic tree. The cutting of that tree must have been an epic tale in itself; now, rock and roots together faced the empty sea and sky. A building stood upon the hewn-off stump; a Fire Marble Dome turned in rusty solitude upon the flat rock to one side.

I'd materialized within the dome, of course, and swiftly made my way along a railed walkway toward a crevice in the rock. There, I found an elevator control that was disturbingly similar to the control on the wahrk gallows, and a puzzle as well. The elevator was shrouded in metal bars, obviously the cage that prevented Catherine from leaving, or anyone from the outside from reaching her. There was also a locking mechanism of sorts, three keys and a lever. Depressing each key in turn elicited a peculiar sound, each different, each oddly mechanistic, a distinct, sharp, metallic clink, a brief rattle, and a high-pitched ping. A lever above was evidently used to engage the combination once it had been entered. I had no idea what the combination might be, of course, so all I could do was pull the handle. The elevator carried me up through the heart of the ancient stump, opening at last on the room I'd glimpsed in the viewer beneath the lake on Plateau Island. Catherine was even more beautiful than I'd thought after my brief glimpse in the viewer, a slim, pale, but regal woman with black hair and dark, wise eyes, strong and defiant even in her captivity. She emerged speaking an alien tongue which I imagined was Rivenese; Gehn's journal had mentioned with some frustration that she spoke only Rivenese to him.

When she saw me, she was obviously taken aback. "You came!" she exclaimed, dark eyes brightening. Then she grew cautious once again. "But how'd you get past Gehn?" she wondered aloud. She glanced about the room, then stepped back. "I know what he is doing. He's watching you! He is waiting for you to make a mistake!" The lady, it was clear, had a long and unhappy knowledge of her captor. Abruptly she came close to the elevator bars, out of sight of Gehn's Survey Room spying eye. "I think I know how to signal Atrus," she whispered. Drawing herself erect once more, she said in regal tones loud enough to reach the ears of unseen listeners, "Go then! If you won't help me, then I have nothing more to say!" Without another word, she turned and strode from the room, passing out onto the railed balcony I'd glimpsed earlier through the viewer.

I wondered if Catherine had assured me that she could signal Atrus and thereby enable us to escape from this dying world, in order to ensure that I would return to free her after I had trapped Atrus's father. Did she really think that I would abandon her, that I would not do everything in my power to get her back in Atrus's arms? The thought sobered me as I manipulated the elevator control to return to the lower level, then walked back across the wind- and spray-swept walkway to the Fire Marble Dome. I knew what I had to do now.

But the very thought terrified me.

During the Myst affair, of course, I'd had my first exposure to Trap Books. Atrus's two errant sons, Achenar and Sirrus, had each been trapped in a different book of the other's devising. The only way for them to escape was if they could convince someone else—they'd hoped it to be me—to touch the image of their face. Touch the image, and I would have been transported into that Trap Book, a kind of cranny in the black emptiness between the universes, and the person trapped within the book would be free.

Many years ago, during a hunting expedition through the ruins of D'ni, I chanced upon a formula for a most unusual type of Book. Unfortunately, due to the fact that my father was then in the habit of confiscating my discoveries, I was forced to leave it behind. Years later, however, as part of my efforts to protect the vulnerable words linked to the Books in my library, I was pleased to find that I could still recall most of the formula, and with little experimentation quickly succeeded in creating one of these devices myself.

The procedure is actually quite simple: by altering key lines of text but slightly, a normal Linking Book's connection can be partially severed, such that anyone who attempts to use the Book will be permanently trapped in the dark void of the Link — that is, unless someone else uses the Book, at which point that person would become trapped, and the first person displaced back into the world.

-- Atrus' Journal

I worked the combination of the Marble Dome, opened the Linking Book within, and stepped through to Gehn's 233rd Age once more, finding myself, again, behind bars. The call button, as promised, had reset itself. I touched it and, in another moment, Gehn reappeared. "I'm relieved you've returned!" he told me. "I thought perhaps you decided against it."

Again, he offered me the open page of the Trap Book, and I laid my hand unhesitatingly upon the moving image of the caverns of D'ni. A kind of rushing blackness swept around me, swallowing me, engulfing me like a great and hungry wahrk.

When next I could see, I was in a black place. Somewhere above me, the face of Gehn looked down upon my prison, brow furrowed, as if searching. While I could see him looking down at the open page of the book, I knew that he was seeing, not me, but the false image of D'ni. I could almost hear the thought uppermost in his mind. *Has he done it? Has he gone through?* He hesitated a moment longer, and then his hand, vast and black, descended upon my one tiny window of light.

The whirling, rushing sensation returned; for an instant, it seemed I was passing somehow *through* Gehn as he fell into my former prison, and I imagined—I pray it was imagination only!—his despairing shriek as he realized the magnitude of his error.

And then I was in the 233rd Age once more, standing now *outside* the bars of my former prison.

And Gehn lay within the book in my hand.

I wasted no time in exploring Gehn's refuge. A switch on the window ledge lowered the bars of the cage, giving me access to all of the Linking Books. This, I imagined, was the "office" of which Catherine had spoken. The combination to her prison door must be hidden here somewhere.

It took me a long and nearly heartbreaking search to find it, but find it I did, in a strange and dull-silvery orb that appeared to be a watch of some kind, lying on the bedside table in his sleeping quarters one level below the main room. When I opened the device, I heard a pattern of clicks, rattles, and pings, each sound identical to the separate sounds I'd heard upon depressing the keys at Catherine's elevator. Listening several times, I memorized the pattern, then swiftly returned upstairs, and linked through to Catherine's Island. In moments more, I was pressing the keys in the proper order, then moving the unlock lever above. The bars rotated aside and the elevator ascended. Catherine scarcely glanced at me as she realized she was free, but dashed into the elevator beside me, pulling on the lever to send us back down, to freedom. "You did it!" she exclaimed, studying the Trap Book I showed her. "We're all free! You captured Gehn!"

Then her face clouded once more. "I'll have to get the villagers to safety as soon as possible," she told me in hushed, urgent tones. "You go back to Temple Island and reopen the Fissure. I know it's risky, but it's the only way to signal Atrus."

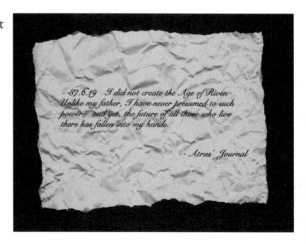

-87.6.19 I did not create the Age of Riven—Unlike my father, I have never presumed to such power—and yet, the future of all those who live there has fallen into my hands.

-- Atrus' Journal

The Fissure! But how…?

"Don't forget," she said. "The portal combination's in my journal. Good luck."

And then she was gone. By the time I reached the Fire Marble Dome, it was closed and turning once more, indicating that she had already passed through.

Certain now of the task before me, I opened the dome and returned to Gehn's world, then linked through to Temple Island. Hurrying now, the end almost within sight, I raced through the Great Golden Dome to the Gate Room, then manipulated the controls until I could step through to the second position, the one I'd discovered so long before when I'd first begun my tentative explorations of this place. The valve was as I'd left it; I turned it, providing steam for the telescope mechanism outside. I exited the Gate Room by way of the cave and wiggled beneath the wooden gate, then ran as fast as I could up the stone steps and down once again, rounding the Gate Room hill to arrive where my adventure on Riven had begun, days before. With power to the telescope switched on, the lever to the side set the mechanism to go up or down, and the button activated it. Using Catherine's journal, I swiftly translated the D'ni numbers she'd scribbled down on one of the pages and opened the round metal hatch.

I took a moment, with the hatch open, to peer through the telescope's eyepiece.

I was looking down into a great crevice in the solid earth… and I was looking at stars.

Stars! The eyepiece was filled with them in their uncountable multitudes.

The Star Fissure indeed. This was, then, the fissure into which Atrus had hurled his Myst Book long ago. The book that had brought me first to Myst and now to the edge of the star-filled precipice on Riven.

I found and opened a locking pin that would block the telescope's descent, set the lever at the down position, and pressed and held the green button. With a grinding of gears, the telescope descended, the narrow tip at the bottom dropping toward that glass plate that stood between Riven's atmosphere, and the star-strewn glory beyond.

Once, in a biology class in school many years before, I'd committed the unpardonable sin of focusing my microscope's objective lens *down*, toward the slide and the hapless paramecia performing their mindless acrobatics within a drop of water from a hay infusion jar. The slide had cracked with a loud report, and I'd received a stiff lecture from my teacher on the delicacy of a microscope's objective lens.

Now I was trying to repeat that unfortunate experiment, but on the scale of an entire world.

After I pressed the button one last time, the tip of the telescope touched the glass, and for an age-long moment, nothing happened.

And then the glass shattered.

The report was far louder than the cracking of my microscope slide in school. It was a thunderclap of sound, one echoed seconds later by an answering stroke from the heavens. The wind howled, funneling down into the fissure, which within seconds had swallowed the steel plating roofing it over, the telescope support braces, and then the entire telescope.

The ground quaked and rocked. Reeling back against the cliff, to which I attempted to cling for safety, I watched as the crevice opened, a yawning, gaping gash in the ground. Overhead, the sky had turned green-black, as clouds raced through what seconds before had been a peaceful and sunny sky. The huge, metal dagger standing point-down in the nearby rocks toppled, falling full length within the crack, and I found myself hoping with just a touch of hysteria that it didn't hit anyone when it landed and cleave them in two.

Had I misunderstood? Was *this* what Catherine had asked me to do?

At the cylindrical chamber within which I'd first appeared on Riven an age or two ago, Atrus materialized. Sprinting across the convulsing ground, he faced me, shouting to be heard above the roar of the wind. "Where's Catherine! Where's the Book?"

I had no answer for the question that must have been uppermost in his mind. He reached for the Trap Book in my hand, opened it, and studied it a moment.

"Atrus?" It was Catherine, appearing from behind the shuddering mountain. Atrus whirled at her voice, then ran to her. They embraced as an Age crumbled around them.

"The villagers are safe in the Rebel Age," she told me a moment later. "I thank you."

"As do I," Atrus added. He leaned closer, speaking intently. "You have accomplished more than I could have hoped for." He glanced at Catherine. "You've given me back… my life."

He opened the linking book for Catherine. She smiled at me, briefly, then touched its page, fading from view like a wind-shredded mist.

Atrus held the book open, above the star-filled, wind-howling gash in the earth. "Perhaps we'll meet again someday. Goodbye, my friend."

He touched the book and vanished, as had Catherine. Unsupported now, the book toppled into the Star Fissure.

For a panicked moment, I wondered if Atrus had abandoned me to the disintegrating Age of Riven, but then a kind of peace suffused my being, even as the ledge crumbled beneath my feet and I toppled forward into the fissure, following the downward spinning Link Book into the sea of stars. The space beneath me was neither empty nor hostile; once before, the Myst linking book had found its way through to my Earth. I knew with calm certainty that I would now follow that same path.

I was going home.

Still, as I tumbled gently through Night Everlasting, I couldn't help but clutch at Atrus's final words.

Perhaps we'll meet again someday… in another world…

…in another Age.

The End

CHAPTER SIX
Puzzles and Problems: The Solutions

This is a WAHRK chapter. It lists each of the major problems and puzzles of Riven and presents all of the solutions, with *no* attempt at concealing them. DON'T READ THIS CHAPTER, don't even page through it, if you want to have a chance of solving Riven's puzzles on your own!

The Gate Room

▶ The Gate Room is a five-sided chamber that rotates 72 degrees clockwise each time you press one of the rotation buttons at the outer doorways.

▶ The Gate Room has two open doorways. It rotates within a chamber that has five possible gateways. As the inner room turns, it opens connections between a different pair of gateways with each rotation.

▶ The geometry of the gate room looks like the following:

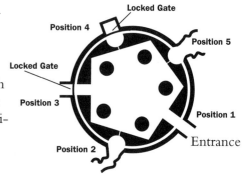

▶ The five possible gateways are labeled 1 through 5. Position 1 is the first gate, on the southeast wall, which you encounter at the beginning of the game. The first time you enter the room, the open doors connect positions 1 and 3.

▶ Each time you press the rotation button, the inner chamber turns by one of its five sides.

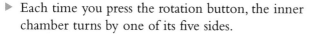

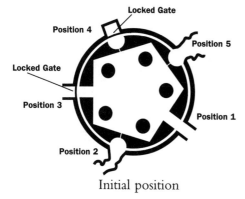

Initial position

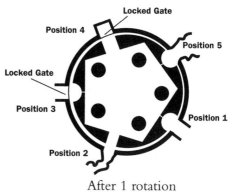

After 1 rotation

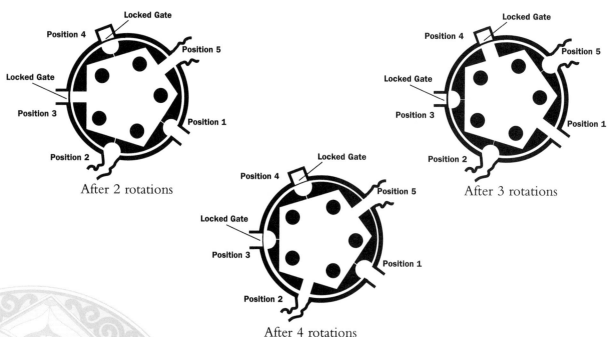

After 2 rotations

After 3 rotations

After 4 rotations

▶ From position 1, you can access position 3. If you rotate the room three times, you can access position 4.

▶ When you first encounter the Gate Room, lowered grates at positions 3 and 4 block your access to the only two doors you can reach from position 1. The switch to raise the grate at position 4 is at position 2, and the one to raise the position 3 grate is at position 4. You need to access one of the other positions and go through in order to rotate the room again and gain access to the other gates.

▶ To do this, first press the rotation button at position 1 four times to open the doorways at 5 and 2. (You are heading for position 5, which is the one position that does *not* have a rotation button.) Then follow the outside path around and down to the wooden gate on the east side of the building. Click on the ground beneath the locked gate to crawl underneath and access the cave beyond. Go up through the cave to the open doorway. Go through to position 2, where you will find the switch that raises the grate at position 4, as well as the power valve for turning on the power to the telescope outside.

▶ From position 2, rotate the inner room twice to align open doors at positions 2 and 4. Go through to 4 where you will find the switch to raise the grate that blocks position 3. A door locked from the other side prevents you from going to position 4. Instead, from position 4, rotate the room two more times to connect positions 4 and 1. Go through to 1 and rotate twice. This opens the doors at 1 and 3, just as they were when you first entered this room. However, now the grate at 3 is raised, which enables you to continue your explorations in that direction.

The Magnetic Tram

▶ The trams on Riven are fairly straightforward and easy to figure out. A few points need to be kept in mind.

▶ The knob to the side of the main, central control rotates the car 180 degrees. Move it to the right or left to place the tram in position to go.

▶ The lever at the center makes the tram go. Once this switch is thrown, travel is automatic.

▶ Near each tram station is a silver sphere atop a stand or pedestal with a blue button or press-plate at the top. Press this to call a tram if none is waiting for you at the station.

▶ At Plateau Island, use the tram's rotation to allow you to turn in place, thereby reaching a door that is otherwise inaccessible.

The Submarine

▶ To lower the submarine into the water, follow the paths and piers counterclockwise around Village Lake on Jungle Island until you reach the Village. Continue to climb ladders and follow the one path you can until you reach the highest point beyond the Village, a ceremonial area where the submarine has been raised on a kind of elevator platform. Throw the lever to lower the sub into the water.

▶ Proceed back the way you came, down the ladders to the pier, and then clockwise around the lake, past the Jungle, past the clear-cut, past the rope bridge, down the stone steps past Sunner Rock, and then through a tunnel to emerge once again above the island's central lake. Go down the ladder beyond the Beetle Pool, and follow ladders and paths as far as you can go until you reach the ladder that leads into the submarine.

▶ Note that the submarine's stopping points are located in literal holes in the water. Some quirk of Gehn's technology or the physical laws of this universe enable water here to be shaped at will, creating holes and other peculiar, watery constructs. By studying the surface of the central lake from some elevated vantage point, you can deduce where the submarine stopping places are located.

▶ The submarine controls are simple. The rotating lever turns the sub around. The lever at the bottom can be moved left or right, and determines which fork in the tracks you will take when you move forward across a switch or track crossing. The lever to the right moves the sub forward to the next decision point.

▶ The submarine moves on wheels along an underwater track. The track configuration is as follows:

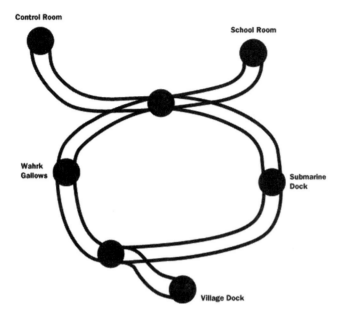

Control Room

School Room

Wahrk Gallows

Submarine Dock

Village Dock

▶ To enter or leave the submarine, a ladder must be lowered from an access pier above the water. The first time you enter the sub, only the ladders at the sub dock and the control tower are lowered. You must go from the sub dock to the tower dock, leave the sub, and then climb a high ladder up the cliff to the control room in order to raise the levers that lower the other three ladders.

▶ With all the ladders down, you can access any of the five sites around the lake. From the sub dock and the village pier, you can leave the submarine and continue your travels elsewhere; the control tower and the school room, while important, are dead ends. Once you leave, you can only return to the sub.

▶ The Wahrk Gallows is a special case. The first time you leave the sub, you can walk around the open base of the gallows, but you will be unable to go anywhere else. Pulling the triangular handle on the chain lowers a bar on a rope, but you cannot reach it and after a moment or two, the rope automatically rises again. After finding your way to Gehn's Throne high above the Wahrk Gallows, you can close the base of the gallows, return to the gallows by submarine, lower the bar and ride it to the top, and find a ladder that you can lower to the lakeside walkway. When this task is complete, you can leave your sub at the gallows and continue your explorations elsewhere as well.

The Wahrk Idol

▶ At the end of a path in the jungle is a huge, brightly painted wooden construction that appears to be some kind of idol or religious totem designed to look like a wahrk. The path seems to end there.

▶ While standing between two posts or decorations with rounded tops, face the idol. Touch the top of the right-hand post. This raises a switch that opens the wahrk idol's mouth.

▶ Follow the stairs into the idol. A lever closes the mouth or opens it again. Beyond that point, an elevator can take you up to the jungle catwalks, Gehn's Throne, and the island's Fire Marble Dome, or down to the mag-tram that can transport you to Plateau Island.

▶ You can first penetrate the idol when you arrive from Plateau Island. When you emerge from the idol's mouth, you will see the raised switch on the post to your left. Clicking on the switch closes the idol's mouth once more.

The Wahrk Gallows

▶ To get to the Moiety Age, you must get past the Wahrk Gallows.

▶ Use the submarine to reach the Control Tower, which is one stop beyond the gallows (moving clockwise around the lake). In the Control Tower, raise all the levers to lower all of the ladders.

▶ When you learn the secret of the Wahrk Idol, follow the catwalk past the Jungle Island Fire Marble Dome and find the tower housing Gehn's Throne Room. Throw the left-hand lever to raise the Throne, and then throw the right-hand lever to close the base of the Wahrk Gallows, allowing access across the base.

▶ Use the submarine to reach the gallows and exit there. Cross to the center of the (now closed) base and pull the triangular handle on a chain.

▶ A bar hanging from a rope will lower. Grab the bar and ride it up to the top.

▶ From here, you can lower a ladder to the pier to ensure future access. You can also find the prison cell and its prisoner. From here, you can find your way through a secret passage to the Moiety Gateway Room.

D'ni Numbers

▶ Learn how to count in fluent D'ni by using the sub to reach the school room, which is one stop beyond the Control Tower. Play the wahrk counting game to learn the first 10 digits. Use the patterns you find here to deduce the numbers from 11 through 25.

▶ The D'ni use a base five counting system. In the base 10 system, which we use, we have distinct numerals for 1 through 9, with 10 represented as a 1 with a zero to the right of it to show a 1 in the tens' place. Count up another 10, and 20 is written as a 2 with a zero to the right to put it in the tens' place. In the D'ni system, they have unique symbols for 1 through 4; they then build on these through rotation and combination to create higher numerals.

▶ The D'ni numerals from 1 to 5 are:

| 1 | 2 | 3 | 4 | 5 |

Note that 5 is, in effect, a 1 rotated 90 degrees counterclockwise. (Yes, it could *also* have been rotated clockwise, but bear with us!)

▶ The numerals 6 through 9 are created by combining 5 plus one of the first 4 numerals. Thus, 9 is 5 + 4.

▶ The numeral 10 is a 2 rotated 90 degrees counterclockwise.

| 6 | 7 | 8 | 9 | 10 |

▶ The numerals 11 through 14 are comprised by combining 10 plus one of the first four numerals. Thus 12 is 10 + 2.

▶ The number 15 is made by rotating a 3 counterclockwise 90 degrees.

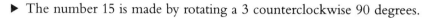

| 11 | 12 | 13 | 14 | 15 |

▶ The numerals 16 through 19 are made by combining 15 plus one of the first four numerals. Thus 18 is 15 + 3. Note that two of the lines in the figure are contiguous and look like a single line.

▶ The number 20 is a 4 rotated 90 degrees counterclockwise.

| 16 | 17 | 18 | 19 | 20 |

▶ The numerals 21 through 24 are made by combining 20 with one of the first four numerals: 21 is 20 + 1.

▶ The symbol for 25 is different.

| 21 | 22 | 23 | 24 | 25 |

▶ The first 25 D'ni numerals, then, are written as follows:

▶ A string of numbers, as for a five-digit code, would have the numerals written side by side. For example, the code string 3 - 7 - 8 - 11 - 22 would be written:

| 3 | 7 | 8 | 11 | 22 |

▶ While exploring Riven, you should always be on the lookout for D'ni numerals. They always mean something important!

The Boiler

▶ The boiler is the first large structure you see on the beach when you arrive on Crater Island. It is used to boil wood chips (from logs transported from Jungle Island and reduced to splinters in the chipper) to create pulp for making paper, a vital component in Gehn's bookmaking experiments.

▶ You must solve the Boiler Puzzle to gain access to the boiler tank, cross a raised floor grating to a ladder leading down a drain in the center, and eventually reach the mountaintop. It's on this mountaintop where you can attempt to gain access to Gehn's laboratory.

▶ The boiler is powered from a pipe that extends into the center of the lake. To power the boiler and operate the controls, you must follow the walkway out to the middle of the lake and set the steam valve lever to the middle of the three possible positions.

▶ You must set the boiler controls a certain way in order to gain access to the tank's interior and the ladder in the center.

▶ The first control is on the left of the walkway around the boiler building as you approach the main controls; a valve lever can be set to one of two positions. The higher/farther position powers the water pumps for filling and emptying the boiler. The lower/nearer position powers the grating.

▶ The main controls consist of a wheel to the left which fills or drains the tank, a lever to the right which turns the furnace on or off, and a switch at the upper right that raises or lowers a grate inside the tank.

▶ To enter the boiler, the furnace must be turned off. When it's on, you will hear a roar, a red light is visible by the boiler door, and the door itself is locked.

▶ To enter, the tank must be empty. Make sure the power at the "Y junction" is switched to the far/high pipe. Turn the large wheel to move the pipe and watch the water drain away through the vertical glass view port.

▶ To enter the boiler and get across to the ladder, the floor grating must be raised. Make sure the valve at the "Y junction" is set to the nearer/lower branch. Throw the switch at the upper right, and watch the grate rise into position. If the grate was up and you've just lowered it, throw the switch again to reposition it.

▶ With the furnace off, the tank empty, and the grate raised, you can enter the boiler tank and reach the ladder.

Gehn's Laboratory

▶ To reach Gehn's laboratory on Crater Island, you must go through the following steps.

▶ Go through the drain pipe after solving the Boiler Puzzle (see previous section). Emerge on the mountain and follow a path across the rocks and down onto a railed platform on the cliff face.

▶ Open the round hatch, which was locked from underneath. This gives you access to the beach and the boiler again, should you need it.

▶ Go through the double doors and then close them to reveal hidden passageways to left and right.

▶ Follow the right-hand passage as you face the doors from the inside. Find a lever against the rocks and pull it, which turns off the ventilation fans inside. (This walkway also leads to the front of Gehn's lab, which is locked, and then to the West Drawbridge and the Great Golden Dome.)

▶ Return to the double doors and turn left. Follow the steps down to the frog-catching chamber.

▶ With the ventilator fans off, you can click on the grating above the frog trap apparatus to open the shaft and crawl inside.

▶ Follow the ventilator shaft until you come to another opening. Click on the grate to open it and drop into Gehn's lab.

▶ You can now unlock the front door, read Gehn's lab journal, and use the tram out the back door to travel to Plateau Island.

▶ Make sure you read the lab journal and take note of the numerical code inside. You can't take the journal with you.

The Map Table Puzzle

▶ On Plateau Island, you will find a rather fiendish puzzle—it's easy to work, but difficult to interpret. You must solve this puzzle, however, to complete the Marble Puzzle you encounter later.

▶ When you ride the elevator up to the mountaintop, you will have access to two areas: A spot overlooking five plateaus, which represent the five islands of Riven; and a large, circular building, the Map Room, in the center of a lake. The two sites are connected by a path that runs through the elevator and across a narrow walkway that may extend into the lake.

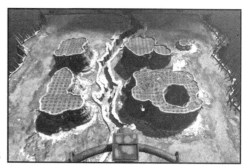

▶ At the overlook, look down to see the control panel, a plate with five buttons, each shaped like the graphic designs representing the five different islands. Push one of the buttons; note how the plateau below the overlook representing that island changes (water flows onto the top, assuming the shape of that island's mountainous terrain). (Water on Riven, as you may have noticed by now, does *not* behave the same way that it does in more mundane universes!)

▶ Cross the path from the overlook to the Map Room. The walkway now extends out to the Map Room.

▶ The Map Table is a large grid divided into a five-by-five array of large squares, 25 squares in all.

▶ One square on the Map Table represents one square in the small island symbol below.

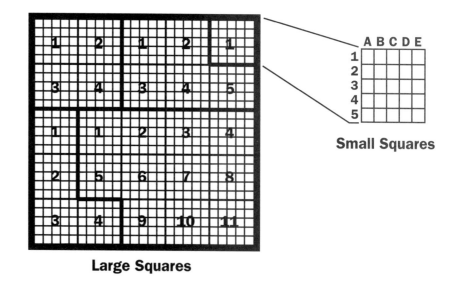

Large Squares

Small Squares

▶ Elsewhere in your travels (on a plaque inside the entrance to the Great Golden Dome, on the mosaic behind one of the beetles in the Gate Room, and on the control panel at the overlook on Plateau Island), you have seen small graphic designs representing the five islands of Riven. You will see them again on the linking books to each of the islands. The array before you—the Map Table—represents the same shapes.

▶ When you press one of the island-shaped buttons at the overlook above the plateaus, that island shows the shape of its terrain with oddly flowing water. At the same time, that particular island is displayed here, in the Map Room.

▶ One of the large squares of the island display will be highlighted in yellow. Press that square, or any other, to access a holographic image of the terrain in that square. Note the blue lines further dividing the terrain into a five-by-five grid of small squares.

▶ You must conclude that the puzzle requires you to note the locations of each of the Fire Marble Domes on the five islands of Riven, one dome for each island. You should be able to make this deduction when you see the Marble Puzzle in the upper level of the Golden Dome, after you see the 25x25 grid and the six colored marbles to the right. (You will only need five of the six marbles, a further twist to this admittedly fiendish puzzle.)

▶ To solve the Map Table Puzzle on Plateau Island, carefully examine each square, and search for identifying terrain features that will enable you to locate the dome locations.

▶ To record your deductions, you must work out some sort of coordinate system. For the purposes of this guide book, we number each of the large squares of each island, starting from the upper left, going left to right and top to bottom.

▶ Next, in each large square, the small squares are identified by labeling the columns across **A**, **B**, **C**, **D**, and **E**, and numbering the rows down **1**, **2**, **3**, **4**, and **5**.

▶ Examine each map carefully, using the handle beneath the map to rotate the map. You are looking for a flat square where the dome could reside. In some cases, there are identifiable terrain features to guide you.

▶ The Fire Marble Dome on Crater Island (in the upper-left corner) is directly beneath a crater or hole in a mountaintop.

▶ The dome on Plateau Island is just behind a narrow, V-shaped cleft in the rock wall of the central lake.

▶ The dome on Temple Island is on a flat piece of land that extends beyond the circle of the Great Dome.

▶ The dome on Jungle Island is located on a cylindrical pillar of stone.

▶ Prison Island's dome is on a spit of land that extends out into the sea at the southeastern edge.

▶ The exact positions can be plotted as follow:

ISLAND	LARGE SQUARE	SMALL SQUARE
Crater Island	1	B4
Plateau Island	4	A2
Temple Island	2	A1
Jungle Island	5	D2
Prison Island	1	B1

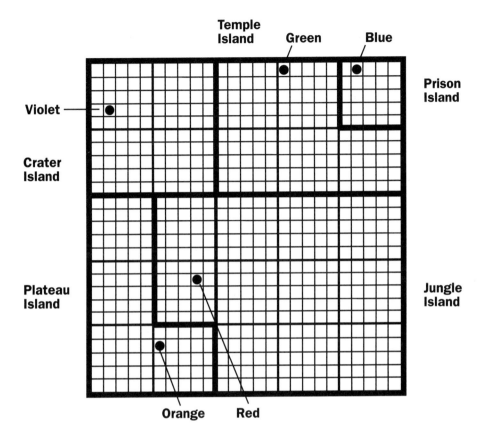

The Moiety Age

▶ You must reach the Moiety Age at some point in your quest in order to recover your Trap Book and to find Catherine's journal.

▶ To open the gateway to the Moiety Age, you must acquire some clues from Jungle Island (plus one missing piece from Plateau Island).

▶ Find the silhouette of a frog near the tram that brings you to Jungle Island. The wooden eye has the D'ni numeral "3" on the back and makes a song like a frog's chirp.

▶ Find the silhouette of a beetle in a stone pool you fill with water on the way to the access ladder at the submarine pen. The wooden eye had the numeral "2" on the back and makes a sound like the whirr-click of a beetle.

▶ Find the silhouette of a wahrk in the rocks on the lagoon past Sunner Rock. The wooden eye has the D'ni numeral "5" and makes a whale-like sound similar to a wahrk. You can confirm this by calling a wahrk and hearing its cry when you are in Gehn's underwater Viewing Chamber on Plateau Island. The wahrk approaches your vantage point if you use the Color Wheel to turn on the red light outside.

▶ Find the fourth eye in the jungle, off the path just below the spot where a large dagger is thrust point-down into the earth. There is no animal silhouette here, but the eye makes the distinctive bark of a sunner, which you have heard if you were able to sneak close to the sunners on their basking rock earlier.

▶ Find the fifth silhouette (that of a fish with a vaguely delta-form shape) in the viewer on Plateau Island in Gehn's underwater Viewing Chamber. Although you may think you see the wooden eye through the viewer, you cannot reach the spot. You must deduce that the number associated with the fish is "1."

▶ When you reach the Moiety Gateway, a room with a circle of 25 stones, each with the graphic image of a different Rivenese life form, you must touch the five stones in the correct sequence.

▶ The images and the sequence are:

Fish   Beetle   Frog   Sunner   Wahrk

▶ If you click on the wrong stone or in the wrong order, nothing will happen. You must touch the stones already moved in reverse order to back out of the mistake, and then begin again with the correct sequence. The stones will also automatically reset when a sixth stone is pressed.

The Fire Marble Domes (First Step)

▶ At some point, you must enter a different age or world, the place Gehn calls his residence, a universe he calls "233." (Gehn has been working on a *lot* of universes! Riven is his fifth!)

▶ You can reach Gehn's world by using the linking book inside any of the Fire Marble Domes you see during your explorations.

▶ To open a rotating Fire Marble Dome, you must approach one of the kinetoscopes facing the dome and look through the eyepiece.

▶ As you look through the eyepiece, the rotating shutter creates a kind of animation, enabling you to see the changing symbols on the rotating dome blend into a kind of movie. One of the symbols, however, is marked in yellow; you will see it flash this color as it goes past.

▶ Click the button on top of the kinetoscope to catch the yellow symbol as it appears. This will take some practice and several tries, but keep at it. When you click on the correct symbol, both the rotating shutter and the dome stop spinning. The dome will then open, and for just an instant, you will see the linking book inside. Then an inner dome will lock shut, a second puzzle that you must solve in order to link with Gehn's world.

▶ Sketch or otherwise note the symbol that opens each dome, and remember which island you found it on. The symbols refer to specific colors; you must know what color goes with which island in order to solve the Marble Puzzle later on.

▶ The kinetoscope for the Fire Marble Dome on Geographical Plateau Island is broken. You can stop that dome by simply clicking on the switch rapidly—basically, just click the mouse as fast as you can—and catching the appropriate symbol randomly. This method, incidentally, can be used on *any* of the domes, should you have trouble catching the correct symbol as it flashes past. When you hit it, you will hear a change in the sound made by the rotating shutter, and the device will spin down. A moment later, the dome will open.

▶ Because the kinetoscope is broken, you must determine the correct symbol for the Plateau Island by careful observation of the dome while it is still spinning.

The Fire Marble Domes (Second Step)

▶ To reach the linking book inside a Fire Marble Dome, you must get the correct five-digit code and use it to position the sliders along the scale on the inner dome lock. When the sliders are correctly positioned, push the button. The sliders will move all the way to the left and the dome will open. If the setting is wrong, the sliders move to the left, but nothing else happens. You can then try again.

▶ The code is located in Gehn's lab journal in his laboratory on Crater Island. The code is different each time you play Riven.

▶ The code is a string of five D'ni numerals, but some will be higher than 10. Because the Wahrk Gallows toy in the schoolroom only teaches you the numerals through 10, you must figure out how the numbering system works in order to translate higher numbers.

If you have trouble, consult the section earlier in this chapter on D'ni numerals.

▶ After entering the correct combination and pushing the button, the inner shield raises and you can access the book. The book will not transport you to Gehn's world, however, unless you have also solved the Marble Puzzle, described earlier in this chapter, and provided the books with power.

▶ The scale on the lock has 25 positions, marked off by fives. Move the right-most slider to the point on the scale corresponding to the highest, right-most number of the code. Move the next slider in line to the next highest number, the second from the right. Continue down the list of numbers, until the last, left-most slider is placed on the last, left-most number in the line.

▶ When you use the Linking Book inside the dome, you will arrive in Gehn's residence in Age 233 (or in D'ni notation, 98). When you use a Linking Book from this location to a specific island, you will arrive inside the Fire Marble Dome of that island. To exit the dome, move back from the book and click on the button you see on the floor to the right of the book. The dome will open and you can step out.

The Marble Puzzle

▶ The solution to the Marble Puzzle requires that you solve the Map Table Puzzle on Plateau Island, described earlier in this chapter.

▶ Each of the symbols associated with a different Fire Marble Dome (the symbols used to open the dome with its kinetoscope) represents a color. The colors and symbols, with their respective islands, are as follows:

COLOR	ISLAND
Green	Temple Island
Red	Jungle Island
Violet	Crater Island
Orange	Plateau Island
Blue	Prison Island
Yellow	None

Note that you must guess at the color for the Prison Island, because you won't be able to reach that Fire Marble Dome until *after* you have solved the Marble Puzzle. Note, too, that you must guess at the color associated with the Crater Island symbol, because that light (purple) is broken on the Color Wheel.

▶ The Marble Puzzle array, which is obviously based on the map array on Plateau Island, must be mentally divided into the graphic logos for the five islands.

▶ Each large island square is numbered, running left to right, top to bottom.

▶ Each large island square is further divided into a five-by-five grid. For simplicity, mentally label the vertical columns of each **A**, **B**, **C**, **D**, and **E**, going left to right, and the horizontal rows **1**, **2**, **3**, **4**, and **5**, going top to bottom.

▶ The proper marble placement for each island is as follows:

ISLAND	COLOR	LARGE SQUARE	COORDINATES
Crater Island	Purple	1	B4
Temple Island	Green	2	A1
Prison Island	Blue	1	B1
Plateau Island	Orange	4	A2
Jungle Island	Red	5	D2

▶ When the marbles are properly placed, move the lever on the wall, and then press the white button. An explosion of air from beneath the marble press signals that power has been provided to the linking books.

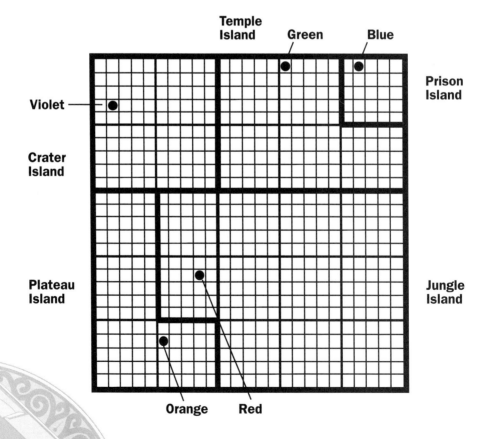

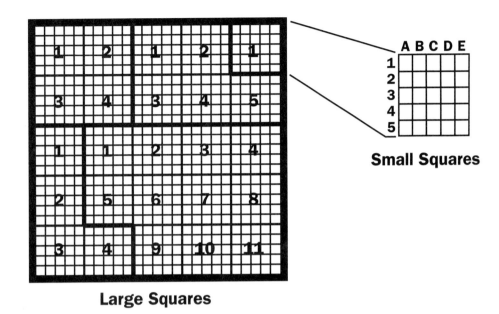

Large Squares

Small Squares

Trapping Gehn

▶ You need the Trap Book Atrus gave you to capture Gehn. It was taken from you when you first arrived in Riven. To get it back, you must solve the puzzle of the Moiety Gateway, enter the Rebel Age, and get the trap book from Nelah, one of Catherine's allies.

▶ While you are behind bars in Gehn's residence, Gehn will take the book, which he thinks is a gateway to the world of D'ni. After considering going through, he reconsiders and asks *you* to go through first.

▶ Although at first glance this seems to be suicide, it is in fact what you must do. Touch the image on the book, and you will find yourself trapped inside. You will see Gehn looking at you, but he is in fact seeing a moving image of the subterranean world of D'ni. After a moment, he will touch the image and follow you in.

▶ If you played Myst, you already know how Trap Books work. When Gehn touches the image, he trades places with you. He is now inside the book, while you are in his home, free to explore *outside* the bars of your cage.

WARNING! DON'T TOUCH THE IMAGE IN THE BOOK AGAIN, OR YOU WILL ONCE AGAIN TRADE PLACES WITH GEHN—THIS TIME PERMANENTLY!

Releasing Catherine

▶ You can reach Catherine's island only through the linking book in Gehn's residence. First, either Gehn must turn the power on to all of the books before you trap him, or you must turn the power on after you trap him.

▶ Trap Gehn by entering the Trap Book yourself. When he follows, you exchange places with him, trapping him in the book and leaving you outside the cage.

▶ Go to the ladder leading down to Gehn's bed chamber. Go to his bed-side table and open the gray sphere, which is a kind of timepiece. As it opens, note the progression of clinking sounds.

▶ Return upstairs and find the lever that lowers the cage around the linking book's access.

▶ Go to Catherine's island using the linking book with the single square. Enter the same sequence of sounds you heard from Gehn's watch using the three keys in the elevator, and then pull the lever.

▶ The bars will open, the elevator will rise, and Catherine, freed at last, will join you.

The Telescope

▶ Get the code of five D'ni numbers from Catherine's journal.

▶ Make sure the valve located in the cavern at Position 2 is turned to point to the right, providing power to the telescope assembly.

▶ Enter the numbers to open the hatch on the steel plates beneath the telescope.

▶ Move the pin on the support strut at the left to allow the telescope to go down.

▶ Lower the lever, then press and hold the green button to move the telescope down until the glass is cracked and the Star Fissure is opened.

Things *Not* To Do In Riven

Although Riven is not a violent or combat-oriented game, there are a few things that you should avoid if at all possible. In some cases, you can even get killed.

▶ Do *not* use the trap book yourself when Gehn is not around. You will be trapped there forever, and Atrus will be *very* upset.

▶ When Gehn offers you a chance to touch the trap book image, do *not* continue to refuse him. After three refusals, he will stop wasting time on you, and kill you. Well, what did you expect of someone who smokes frogs and plays God with people's lives?

▶ When you trap Gehn, do *not* touch the image of D'ni again! You will exchange places with him once more, and this time, become trapped forever.

▶ Do *not* power up and operate the telescope before you have trapped Gehn. If you do, Atrus will appear and, moments later, so will Gehn, along with one of his guards. Gehn will kill both Atrus and you.

▶ Do *not* operate the telescope before you rescue Catherine. If you capture Gehn but do not free Catherine, you have won a limited and melancholy victory at best. In this scenario, you and Atrus have survived, but Atrus may never see his wife again, and the Rivenese themselves may all die in a world's collapse. Pity Atrus! He has lost his beloved Catherine, the world he has labored to save, and his father, all at the same time!

CHAPTER SEVEN
Walkthrough: All Revealed

This is a WAHRK chapter. Don't read it, don't even skim through it, unless you want a lot of the fun and mystery of Riven spoiled for you!

This chapter gives away *everything*, without worrying about how or where you get much of the information, and with scarcely a nod toward the rich and atmospheric wonder that is the world of Riven. Follow this outline if you want to get from beginning to end in the shortest and most direct possible time.

A *much* better idea is to play the game and figure out the puzzles for yourself, or at most, with a little help from other chapters in this book! Then look here and compare with this walkthrough how well you did and to see what *other* endings you might have encountered!

Also, with a game like Riven, there is no one right or best way to travel through the various locations or to gather the necessary clues. The order of events in this walkthrough is significantly—and deliberately—different from the order set in Chapter 5, "Walking Through Riven." In most cases, what is important is that you assemble the clues and solve the puzzles, not the order in which you do so.

With that said, let's begin!

The Walkthrough

Temple Island: The Gate Room

▶ When you are released from the cage, check out the mechanism ahead. It's a telescope, but it seems to be pointed at a sealed hatch on a portion of the ground covered by iron plates. Note the lever to the right with a button in the middle—neither works. The mechanism has no power.

▶ Go back toward the cage you arrived in, go to the left, and follow the steps up. Briefly venture out onto the bridge that leads to your right, stop, turn, and look back to see the enormous golden dome behind and to the left of the Gate Room. This is your first goal.

▶ Return back the way you came on the bridge and continue straight into the Gate Room antechamber. Note a button on the wall to your right, and the open door ahead that leads into the Gate Room. Proceed into the Gate Room.

▶ Explore the Gate Room. It is five-sided with two open doors, currently at Positions 1 (where you came in) and 3, which is blocked by a grating. You must open the grating to go through the second doorway at 3, which leads to the giant golden dome. Note the beetles on the pillars. The pull ring at the tail of each beetle reveals a small painting, different for each. A *very* close look at each of the three walls covered with indecipherable writing reveals tiny pinholes through the stone.

▶ To use the Gate Room, you must understand its geometry. There are five possible gateways, numbered for easy discussion, starting at 1 (on the southeast wall, where you entered), and proceeding clockwise around the room, 2, 3, 4, and 5. Pushing any of the rotation buttons outside the Gate Room rotates the room by one wall: 72 degrees.

▶ Return to the antechamber. You begin with open gates aligned at 1 and 3. Push the button on the right to rotate the Gate Room clockwise 72 degrees. At this point, the gate into the room is closed, but you can peek through a small lens in the recess in front of you and see the room's interior.

▶ The room's open gates are now aligned with Positions 2 and 4. Push the rotation button again to turn the gateways to Positions 3 and 5. Push it again to turn the gates to Positions 4 and 1. The gateway in front of you is now open once again. Note that the gate at Position 4 is closed off by a grate.

▶ Push the button to rotate the room one more time. The open gateways should now be at 2 and 5. Return to the path, turn left, and follow the steps down. When you've gone as far as you can, turn left twice to face a locked gate. Click under the gate to go inside. Go up the ladder and across a board. Ahead, note the open door into the Gate Room at Position 5.

▶ Go through the Gate Room and into the cave at Position 2. Throw the steam-valve lever, which turns on the power to the telescope apparatus outside. (You won't need this until the end of the game, but you might as well take care of this little chore now.) Turn around and head back toward the Gate Room. Note the rotation button to the right of the door, and a lever to the left. Throw the lever to raise the grate that closes off Position 4.

▶ Push the rotation button twice to open Positions 2 and 4. Go through the Gate Room to Position 4. The grating is raised now, enabling access to an antechamber at 4, but the way beyond is blocked by a massive door. Obviously, you'll need to go somewhere else to open this door. Turn around to see another handle on the left side of the door. Throw it to lower the grate you originally noticed at Position 3.

▶ Push the rotate button twice to move the openings to Positions 4 and 1. Go across the Gate Room to the main entrance and rotate twice to align Positions 1 and 3. With the grate at Position 3 now raised, cross the room to Position 3.

▶ Go across the bridge to the Great Golden Dome. Note the lever in the dome doorway. Operating the lever does nothing; you will need to restore power. Put the lever back to the position in which you found it.

▶ Enter the giant chamber. Note the sign, which shows island symbols and indicates that this chamber connects with all five. It also shows the catwalk you are standing on, with a missing piece at 5 o'clock. If you look to your right, you can see the missing catwalk section, and what looks like a large wheel on the far side.

▶ Follow the catwalk to the left, and follow a long flight of stairs as you circle halfway around the chamber. Outside, there's a short catwalk extending out from the main walkway, where a vertical pipe is bleeding off steam. Throw the steam valve lever to turn power on to the West Drawbridge (which connects the Golden Dome with Crater Island). Return to the main catwalk and follow it to the left. Note the elevator button on the rock face as you pass, but continue around the outside of the giant dome, passing into and through a rock tunnel. Exit the tunnel and you'll find another steam valve. Throw the lever to restore power to the bridge that connects the giant dome with the Gate Room.

▶ Turn around and head back through the tunnel. As you emerge from the tunnel, notice the button set in the wall to your left. At the moment, it's not operational, but remember it. You may need it later.

▶ Now return to the Golden Dome and go through it up the stairs. At the entrance, throw the lever and watch the bridge raise and extend to a position somewhere above you. Lower the bridge again and return to the Gate Room. Go through to Position 1. You have now solved the Gate Room puzzle.

Temple Island: The Temple

▶ Cross the bridge to the temple area of the island. Go through the entrance and down a passageway. Go to the door on the left of the passageway and enter the Temple Imaging Room. Note the throne in the chamber. The button on the right as you sit in the throne lowers and raises a cage structure over you. The lever on the left probably controls imaging.

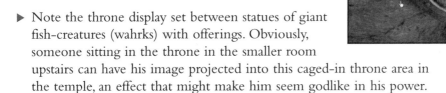

▶ From here you can see two small imaging devices. Go to the device to the left of the door and throw the lever up to open a door in a room filled with pillars (the Temple downstairs). Return to the passageway. Go left and down, entering the Temple by opening a heavy stone door.

▶ Note the throne display set between statues of giant fish-creatures (wahrks) with offerings. Obviously, someone sitting in the throne in the smaller room upstairs can have his image projected into this caged-in throne area in the temple, an effect that might make him seem godlike in his power.

▶ Turn around to see the open temple door, just to the left of the hidden door behind the pillars through which you entered the room. Go through the open door and go right to a mag-lev tramline. Note the blue-lit sphere next to the steps. Press the top to call a tram car to the station when you need one.

▶ Get into the tram. Throw the knob to the left around to the right to rotate the car. Then push the power lever forward to go. You're about to start a wild ride to Jungle Island.

Jungle Island: From the Sunners to the Submarine

▶ When you leave the car, turn to your right. Move forward, and then turn right again. Look until you find a small wooden device painted like a crude eye. Rotate the eye and carefully note the symbol carved on the back. Also, listen to the *creak-chirp* sound the eye makes as it turns. Finally, turn around and go up the stairs directly ahead of you. At the landing, turn around and look back the way you came. Do you see the outline of the tunnel mouth? It's shaped somewhat like a frog with the wooden Eye appearing in the same relative position as the eye of a real frog.

▶ Follow the steps up. Note the blue light sphere—yet another tram call button. Go out of the tunnel and down the stone steps. At the cross path, turn left and keep going down.

▶ Ahead, note some animals sunning on a rock just below the path. As you approach, they raise their heads and make deep, "whuffling" noises. Wait until their heads are down and they stop moving, then approach another step, leaving the path and moving slowly down onto the beach. If you move too quickly (clicking to move when their heads are up), you will scare them off.

▶ If you move cautiously enough, you will reach the beach, where one of the sunners will raise its head and deliver a loud, distinctive bark. Note the sound. You'll need to recall it later.

▶ As long as you're down here, turn right, and then follow the beach around the sunners' lagoon to the left. Note the steps in the distance, but follow the beach to the left as far as you can. Turn around and look at the rocks which form the rough shape of the fish-creature (a wahrk) that you saw in the temple and another wooden Eye.

▶ Move onto the sandbar to reach the Eye. Move it to see another symbol and hear a sound resembling a whale's call. Note the symbol and the sound—both are important.

▶ Return to the beach where you saw the sunners. Go back up the rocks to the path and turn left. Follow the path up the steps you saw from the beach and enter the tunnel. Emerge on a rickety, wooden walkway and follow it to the end. Up ahead you can see a guard tower, where a guard is sounding an alarm.

▶ From here you can look out across an inner lagoon, a lake filling a huge, circular crater. Note a peculiar spherical vehicle on a high ledge to the left. Beyond, you can see a number of strange, spherical buildings.

▶ Go down the ladder and note the dry pool. Turn the petcock on the right to fill the pool. Note the beetle shape formed by the water along with another wooden Eye. Turn the Eye to note both the symbol and a *whirr-click* sound. You'll need to remember them.

▶ Go around Beetle Pool and down the ladder. Follow the walkway to the left. Note what look like holes in the water of Village Lake, and various curious structures around the crater's inner walls. Go into a short tunnel. Find a ladder that leads down into a hole in the water. You can't go any farther from here.

▶ Go back up the ladders, along the walkway, and past the beach all the way to the T-intersection landing. Go past the landing where you came in, and go up the steps in front of you. At the top, cross a rope-and-plank bridge. Note the clear-cut area and jungle beyond with gate and paths. Follow the path to the right when it branches, take the next left, and then turn toward a gate. Note a beetle crawling on the gate post. Click on it to hear the sound it makes, a kind of *whirr-click* you heard previously when you turned the wooden Eye at the beetle-shaped pool. Go through the gate into the forest.

▶ Follow the path. Go down the steps and note the volcanic rumbling in the distance. Go through a tree, past luminous fungus.

▶ Turn around and look for a giant dagger. Turn right at the dagger, follow the steps down, and click on the light. Here's yet another wooden Eye.

▶ Turn the Eye and hear a sunner bark. Note the symbol—there is no animal silhouette associated with this Eye.

▶ Return to the main path and proceed left. See the red glow and hear the rumble again. Take the left-hand path at the Y intersection. Go through the gate, turn left, and up the steps to find yourself back in the clear-cut on what had been the left path when you first approached this area. Go back to the gate. Note the turning fire marble. Go back to the Y intersection. Take the left path (the right path when you first approached this Y intersection). Go along the walkway and down.

▶ Ahead, you can see a giant wahrk idol at the end of the path. There is a cunningly hidden switch on top of the post to the right. Click here to raise the switch and open the wahrk idol's mouth, revealing steps that lead up.

▶ Follow the steps and note the tram call and a wooden elevator. Turn around to find the lever that closes the wahrk idol's mouth. Turn back and enter the elevator. Go down, turn around, and go through to another tramcar station. Return to the elevator and go up two levels, above the level where you entered the idol's mouth.

▶ Emerge from the elevator on a catwalk high above the forest floor. Follow the walkway around to the right. Go past a branching to the right to reach a rotating fire marble dome.

▶ Examine the dome carefully. You'll see these things on every island you visit. Note the symbols flickering past on the rotating dome, and note that one seems to be marked in yellow.

▶ Go back to the branch you passed earlier and follow it to a device facing the dome called a kinetoscope. Watch the changing symbols through the eyepiece; click the button on top when the yellow symbol appears in the viewer. (NOTE: If you have trouble catching it at just the right moment, rapidly click the mouse button. Sooner or later, you'll get it.) The device will stop rotating, as will the large dome. Note the symbol that opened the dome; you'll need to recognize it later.

▶ Go to the now open Fire Marble Dome. Look through the circular window and note what looks like a book inside. Move the sliders and press the button. Nothing happens; obviously, you need to learn a code to open the dome further.

▶ Turn around and exit the dome, turning left to climb a flight of steps to a tower. Open the door and go inside. Note the wahrk skull chair.

▶ When you are seated in the throne, the left handle raises and turns the throne, moving it up to a position from which you can look down on Village Lake. Almost directly below is a circular platform beneath a high tower—it's the Wahrk Gallows, a place of bloody execution.

▶ Turn the right handle to close the bottom platform on the gallows. Note the tracks underneath the water in the lake.

▶ Move the left handle to go back down and leave the room. Go out and back along the walkways to the elevator. Go down one level to the wahrk idol. Open the lever and exit.

▶ Go along the path, toward the tunnel beneath the marble dome, and emerge to see a native child run away from you. Go to the Y intersection and take the right path. Go up the steps and through the gate. Turn right on the catwalk.

▶ Follow the catwalk around to the inside wall of Village Lake. Note a small island above the surface with something that might be a telescope or imaging lens on it. Approach the village of dried mud spheres. Climb the ladders and cross a narrow plank to a house. (If you like, click on the star-shaped doorknocker, and get a glimpse of someone who obviously doesn't want to talk to strangers.)

▶ Follow the walkway to the left, going up a ladder and along the catwalk. Approach a spherical, mechanical contraption, otherwise known as the submarine. Throw the lever on the left to lower the sub into the water. Note the ceremonial area, where large creatures (wahrks, perhaps?) are cut up and their flesh hung up to dry.

▶ Return along the walkways and ladders. In front of the house with the plank, look into the lagoon and see the sub now resting in a hole in the water on the underwater tracks.

▶ Follow the walkway back around the lake, past the gate to the Fire Marble Dome, and up and out past the clear-cut. Cross the rope bridge, go back down past the now-empty Sunner Rock, and follow the paths and ladders past the Beetle Pool and down to the last ladder, which now gives you access to the lowered submarine. You're now ready for a drive around the bottom of Village Lake.

Jungle Island: The Submarine Circuit

▶ Determine how the controls work. The turning handle at the center makes the sub change direction; the lever at the bottom determines which track (left or right) the sub will take at the next track junction; the lever to the right moves the vehicle forward to the next siding or decision point. The gauge at the top right shows when the sub is powered and ready to move.

▶ Turn the sub around, and then move forward twice. Look up, open the hatch, and climb the ladder to the Ladder Control Room.

▶ You will find three lever handles that are down, two that are up. Throw the three handles so that all are up. This extends all submarine access ladder bridges around the lake.

- Return to the sub and turn it around. Go forward onto the main track, and then left at the next siding. Exit the sub and follow the path into the village school room.

- There are several things of interest here, including a cage with a turn-crank that projects a 3-D holograph of Gehn. Turn the crank and get a feel for his evident enjoyment in playing God.

- Go to the wahrk hangman game. Moving the ring at the base accesses a random symbol and lowers one of the two hanging figures a random distance toward the waiting wahrk at the bottom.

- The symbols, you now realize, are numbers. You can learn what symbol represents which number by counting the clicks with each turn. Play the game until you have learned all of the D'ni numbers from 1 to 10.

- What do you think of a world where the children play games that randomly sacrifice victims to hungry monsters? Remember, Gehn *rules* this world!

- You now know that the symbols you've been finding behind the wooden Eyes are numbers. The Eye at the frog shape near the tram station was numbered 3. The Eye on the stones that looked like a wahrk was numbered 5. The Eye in the jungle that played the sunner bark was numbered 4. The Eye in the Beetle Pool was numbered 2. This gives you a useful series: Beetle = 2. Frog = 3. Sunner = 4. Wahrk = 5. You don't know what animal is number 1, nor do you know yet what the sequence signifies.

- Return to the sub. Reverse its direction and go forward one. Make sure the left track is selected, and then go forward once more. Exit the sub at the Wahrk Gallows.

- Cross to the center of the gallows. Pull the triangular hanging handle to lower a bar. Click on the bar to carry yourself up to the top of the gallows. Pass between the wahrk skulls toward a barred, circular portal. Look inside to see a native being held captive.

Jungle Island: Find the Gateway to the Moiety Age

▶ Turn right and follow the walkway to a star-shaped control in the rock. Activate the control and watch the portal open. The native is gone, vanished, it seems, into thin air.

▶ Click on the drainage grate on the floor. Click on the dirty water beneath the grating to open a secret panel in the back wall of the cell. Go through the opening.

▶ Go into the tunnel and hear the door close behind you. Seven clicks in the darkness takes you to a light.

▶ Click on the branch on the left to turn on a light. Turn around and go up to where you can just see another light. Touch the bulb to turn it on and extend the light further. Move ahead one and touch another light. Move ahead one more to see a door. Move ahead one more and touch the light, then turn to see the door on the right. Opening the door to the right closes the door to the left. Follow the new passage.

▶ Enter a circle of 25 stone pillars decorated with graphic animal totems. At this point, you do not have enough information to solve the totem puzzle. The sequence Beetle = 2, Frog = 3, Sunner = 4, and Wahrk = 5 may apply here, but you still don't know what the first symbol is. You *could* try solving it by brute force, trying one animal followed by the four you know in sequence and then resetting the whole thing and starting all over with another animal as 1, and another, and another... There is a better way, however; leave it for now.

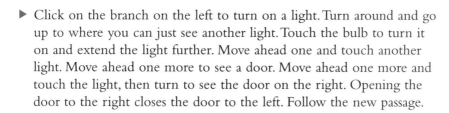

▶ Return up the passage and head toward the secret door in the prison cell. Pull the handle on the ground to the right to open the secret door. Return through the empty prison cell.

▶ Go right out of the prison door and follow the catwalk. Click on the ladder to lower it to the lower level of the catwalk. Climb down the ladder, turn around, and follow the catwalk back clockwise around the lagoon.

▶ Continue along the path and out the gate into the clear-cut area. Take a left, followed by a right to a square tunnel, and go down the tunnel to the logging car ride. Pull the handle on the left to start the car.

Crater Island

▶ Arrive at Crater Island and get dumped into a log chipper. Go down the ladder and find the boiler in the distance. Check the ladder behind the chipper on the rock. It leads to a round hatch, which in turn leads to the logging car for a return trip to Jungle Island.

▶ Go past the boiler to the right and follow the beach around the lake counterclockwise to find a very tall, narrow ladder. The ladder leads to a hatchway that's up the side of the cliff. The hatch is locked from this side, so you can't get through. Note the building farther down the cliff. This is Gehn's laboratory, your eventual goal.

▶ Go to the long, narrow pier that extends into the middle of the lake. There you will find a valve handle with three possible positions. Turning it to the position farthest to the left powers the log chipper. Turning it to the middle position powers the boiler. Turning it to the right (the position in which you find it) powers the frog-catching apparatus in a cave near Gehn's laboratory. Set the valve to the middle position.

▶ Return to the boiler and check it out. The door won't open, and there's a red light on outside the door.

▶ Go back around the outside catwalk to the right to find the boiler controls. The first lever at the Y junction controls the routing of power from the pipe leading out to the middle of the lake. The upper (left fork of the Y) lever powers the pumps that fill or drain the boiler. The lower (right fork of the Y) lever powers a grate that can move up or down inside the boiler. Leave the lever on the upper (left) setting.

▶ Turn to the right and examine the boiler controls. The lever at the lower right controls the heat for the boiler. You can hear a roar, as from a furnace. Turn this lever to the upright position and note that the roar stops and the water in the tank stops boiling.

▶ The wheel at the left moves a pipe that enables you to fill or empty the tank with water. Turn the wheel and watch the water level in the tank fall.

▶ A switch to the upper right controls the position of the movable floor grate inside the tank. First, turn to your left and switch the power valve from the upper (left fork) position to the lower (right fork) position. Then face the main controls again and raise the switch to raise the grate.

▶ Return to the boiler door. Note that the red light is now off. Open the door and look inside: A tube or drainage pipe descends through the middle of the floor with a ladder leading down.

▶ Cross the grate and go down into the drain. You will be enveloped in complete darkness. Click five times to see some light ahead. One more click brings you to a ladder leading up. Continue to move toward the light and emerge from a pipe high up on a mountainside above the sea.

▶ Turn left and follow a faint, worn path in the rocks, which goes over the top of the mountain and down toward the island's central lake. Move toward a railing on a balcony resting against the side of the cliff and climb over. Look down and open the round hatch at your feet. The hatch, locked when you tried to open it from underneath, opens to reveal the long, narrow ladder you climbed earlier that leads to the beach.

▶ Face the cliff to see the double doors. Go through the doors and into the mountain. Turn around and deliberately close the doors, revealing two passageways, one to the right, the other to the left, that are cunningly hidden when the doors are open. You will be returning to these doors shortly.

▶ Turn around again and follow the catwalk into the cave. At the end is an elaborate trap apparatus used by Gehn for catching frogs.

▶ Catching a frog is not necessary for winning the game at this point, but if you want you can return to the beach via the ladder outside, go to the power control in the middle of the lake, turn the valve back to the right, and then return to this chamber. Touch the steel sphere at the top to open the trap. Click and drag to move one of the tiny food pellets from the open container on the right to the trip lever in the middle of the trap. Throw the lever at the left to lower the trap. After waiting about a minute, throw the lever again and raise the trap. If the trap hasn't closed, lower it again and wait some more. If the trap has closed, touch the top to open it and note the brightly colored frog inside. Listen to its chirp, which is the same as the chirp you heard at the wooden Eye in the frog silhouette on Jungle Island.

▶ While you're here, look up at the fan. The loud clattering sound you hear is the noise of the fan running. The ventilator shaft beyond leads to Gehn's laboratory, but you can't access it while the fan is running.

▶ Go back up the catwalk to the two open passages you found behind the double doors. Go left and follow the steps down to a chamber with another Fire Marble Dome. Go around the side of the dome and note the lens of a kinetoscope set into the side wall of the cavern, which should give you an idea as to where to find it. Look up at the opening in the roof, a geological curiosity that you must remember later.

▶ Close the door to the Fire Marble Dome chamber to reveal another hidden door to the right. Enter this room, find the kinetoscope, and use it to stop the spinning dome. Note the symbol.

▶ Go back up the stairs, and then go straight ahead past the double doors and into the opposite passage. Follow the walkway and emerge on the previously unreachable catwalk above the lake. Go forward until you find a lever and hear the clattering racket of ventilator fans. Throw the lever to turn off the fans.

▶ Continue to follow the catwalk. The front doors to Gehn's laboratory are locked, so continue to follow the catwalk around a curve, and then onto a long, high bridge spanning the gulf from Crater Island back to the Great Golden Dome. When you reach a lever at a raised draw-bridge, throw the lever to lower the bridge and open the passage between Crater Island and the Golden Dome.

▶ Continue into the dome, and follow the walkway to the left. Pass one open doorway to your left and continue toward the open section of catwalk noted earlier. Turn the large wheel to extend the bridge and complete the walkway back to the Gate Room.

▶ Proceed to the doorway through which you first entered the Golden Dome. Throw the lever handle on the right to raise the end of the bridge between the Gate Room and the Golden Dome to a new posi-tion in the dome somewhere above your head. Leave it there—you'll need access to this higher level from the Gate Room later.

▶ Before you return to Crater Island, turn off at the side passage you passed by earlier. It leads to a high catwalk that goes around the outside of the building to the right, but you are stopped by a gap in the walk-way. Turn around and press the button on the outer wall to the right of the doorway, and you'll see the catwalk restored as the missing section rises into place.

▶ Continue on the path to a heavy door with a lever to the side. Raise the lever to open the door to Position 4 of the Gate Room, the one you couldn't open from the inside before. (This step is not necessary for the game as it has been laid out in this walkthrough, but is presented here for completeness.)

▶ There is one more excursion you can make at this time, and that is to the Temple Island Fire Marble Dome. Head back for the Golden Dome and turn left, following the stairs down to the outer catwalk on the lower level. Stop just before you enter the tunnel and press the button on the wall to your right. This takes you down to a still lower level, where a smooth-walled tunnel leads to a metal stairway heading up to the Fire Marble Dome.

▶ Operate the kinetoscope to determine the yellow symbol associated with this dome, and write it down. You'll need to know it later.

▶ Now return to Crater Island, and go past Gehn's lab, past the switched-off controls for the ventilator fans, and back to the double doors. Go through and down the catwalk straight ahead to the frog-catching chamber. Look up, and then click on the open ventilator duct to climb inside. Follow the shaft until you reach another ventilator grill, and click on the grating to open it. Drop down into Gehn's laboratory.

▶ Check out his lab—this is where he conducts experiments to determine the proper kind of wood with which to make paper, the proper beetles to make ink, and all of the other details necessary for creating the books that link among the infinity of worlds. At another table, note the paraphernalia he uses for dissecting the frogs. An extract from the frogs is placed in small, cylindrical containers and smoked in his elaborate pipe.

▶ Find his lab journal and go through it carefully. Find and record a string of five D'ni numerals. This is the code for opening the inner mechanism of the Fire Marble Domes. At this point, you know the numerals for 1 through 10. You will need to look for patterns within these numerals in order to deduce the translation of any numbers higher than 10.

▶ Note, incidentally, that this code is different each time you play Riven.

▶ Note, also, the wooden Eye on the desk with the lab journal and note the symbol on the reverse side. Read the paper underneath it to find out where it came from… and how Gehn found out about it.

▶ Examine the stove in the center of the room. Pull the lever to open the door and look inside to see a partly burned linking book. It doesn't work. Note that in Gehn's journal he says he burns books in the oven when they don't work. He seems to be having some trouble getting things right.

▶ Go to the front door and open it, unlocking it so it will now open from the outside. Return through the lab, and touch the blue-topped tram-call next to the door. Go to the opposite door and down the steps toward an awaiting tram.

Plateau Island

▶ Ride the tram to Plateau Island. When you arrive, note the door on the opposite side of the tram from the tram's entrance, but don't do anything about it now. Leave the tram, go out the passageway, and climb the steps. Follow the path through some huge, monolithic stones. Approach the titanic building and go up the steps into the portal. Pass the huge, stone plateaus that rise on either side from the surface of a pond. Continue through the crevice in the rock face and enter an elevator.

▶ Turn around, push the button, and go up to the map viewing level. Go forward and look down to the plateaus in the pond you observed earlier, and which are now obviously maps of Riven's five islands.

▶ Look at the control with five buttons shaped like the islands of Riven. Note how pressing one button causes water to flow onto the top of the corresponding island plateau and hump itself into a three-dimensional relief map of that island's topography.

▶ Turn around, walk back the way you came all the way through the elevator to another crater lake. In the middle of the lake is a large structure: the Map Room.

▶ Approach the map chamber. As you cross the causeway, look to the left and note the Fire Marble Dome for Plateau Island turning just beyond a narrow, V-shaped cleft in the rock wall of the crater.

▶ Enter the map chamber. Note that the water maps and plateaus outside correspond to the map currently visible here. Press the yellow square to see a 3-D relief map of that one square. Use the handle at the bottom to rotate the 3-D map so that you can view it from all sides.

▶ Each island is divided into squares similar to patterns seen on Temple Island. For example, Crater Island is represented by four squares arranged in a square, while Plateau Island consists of four squares arranged in an "L" shape.

▶ Each square, when you click on it, can be further divided into a five-by-five square grid. You need to identify where on each 3-D island map that island's Fire Marble Dome is located.

▶ In the case of Crater Island, you must use additional clues, since the dome is underground. Look for the hole or crater that you saw earlier when you looked up inside that island's Fire Marble Dome chamber. The domes on the other islands are easily identified.

▶ Use the five-by-five grids to create coordinates for each dome site. For example, if the columns across are labeled **A**, **B**, **C**, **D**, and **E**, and the rows down are labeled **1**, **2**, **3**, **4**, and **5**, then the coordinates of the dome on Crater Island are B-4. Record all of the dome sites—or your best guesses—for later reference.

▶ Leave the map room and go to the junction of catwalks, turning right. Investigate the dome in the cleft. Note, if you can, the symbol highlighted in color—a circle with a horizontal line.

▶ Go back around the catwalk, and follow its curvature counterclockwise. As you walk, observe the wahrk totems rising from the lake and note their colors: blue (visible from the side of the lake near the dome), yellow, orange, and green (closest to the kinetoscope).

▶ The kinetoscope is broken, the device pushed out of alignment. To open the dome, simply click your mouse button rapidly until the dome stops rotating.

▶ Return to the elevator, and ride it down to the plateau. Walk along the path, noting the three-dimensional water mountains still rising above the last island you examined. Return to the tram. Rotate the tram to get out on the side of the door you noticed when you first arrived. Go through the door.

▶ Walk down an orange-lit passageway. Note the handle with yellow stripes on the left just before the hexagonal-shaped pool. Throw the lever to raise a golden elevator cage. Go inside. Turn around and push the button to close the elevator and descend beneath the surface of the water.

▶ Emerge from the elevator and follow the passageway through caverns and tunnels. Up ahead, you see Gehn's scribe look up, obviously startled, and dash into a side passage. Follow him to arrive at another tram station, just in time to see the scribe making his escape.

▶ Return to the main passage and turn left. Follow it through a portal and up a long, flight of steps to enter Gehn's underwater Survey Room.

▶ Sit in the throne. Push the button on the control panel to the right to rotate and elevate the throne.

▶ Lower the right-hand lever in front of you to bring down the Color Wheel. Look down at the wheel. Note the symbols, some of which are the same as the symbols you've been noting on each of the Fire Marble Domes. Click on either the symbols or the tabs with finger holes to rotate the wheel. Click on the button at the bottom position to turn on an underwater light.

▶ Go through all of the symbols to connect a specific symbol with a color. The lights are located on the underwater portions of the wahrk totems you noticed earlier. One light, the one symbolized by a circle with a vertical line, is broken; you'll need to guess its color.

▶ The vertical eye shape with a dot, a symbol you've not seen thus far, is blue. The circle with a dot is green. The horizontal eye with a dot in the middle is yellow. The circle with a horizontal line is orange. The eye with a vertically aligned slit pupil is red.

▶ When you click on red, your view shifts up. The red light is visible through the glass of the Viewing Chamber. Wait a few moments to see and hear a live wahrk. Apparently, he's trained to appear to get food when the light is on; when he doesn't get food, he leaves. If you want to play with the wahrk's mind, try calling him three more times and watch him get more agitated each time. After his fourth appearance, he will slam into the glass, and then vanish. He will not reappear unless you return considerably later.

▶ Raise the Color Wheel. Pull the lever to lower the left-hand viewer. This one has only two buttons and six tabs with finger holes. Press the button on the left to see a spy-camera view of Catherine in her prison. When this view is active, the finger hole tabs do nothing.

▶ Press the rightmost button to get a camera's view from Village Lake on Jungle Island. Use the tabs to rotate the view.

▶ Note one view that looks like the silhouette of a fish created by a rock cavern and its reflection in the water, which gives the shape of a delta-wing type configuration. Note a white speck at the pointed end and surmise that the shape is the missing fifth animal silhouette, and that the white speck—unreachable—is the silhouette's wooden Eye.

▶ Leave the throne and go down the stairs to the tram car room where you saw the scribe escape. Take the tram car and ride it back to Jungle Island.

The Moiety Age

▶ Leave the tram, go through the open door, and go to the wooden elevator. Ride up one level to the inside of the Jungle Island wahrk idol.

▶ Leave the jungle via the wooden gate and turn right. Follow the wooden catwalk through the blue-lit cavern and out to the lakeside, where a ladder was lowered earlier. Climb up the ladder, go to the prison cell, and go inside. Open the drain grate, pull the ring, open the secret door, and descend into the cavern. Go down the tunnel to the side passage and the room with 25 stones and animal totems.

▶ Touch the stones in the following order: delta-shaped fish, beetle, frog, sunner, and wahrk. This drains the water from the far wall and provides access to the Moiety universe by opening a ledge with an open book. Touch the screen to see the other universe; click to go through.

Fish   Beetle   Frog   Sunner   Wahrk

▶ Enter the room behind you, where a strange idol is on display. Approach the idol to examine it more closely. Quickly turn to see Moiety rebels shoot at you with a blowgun dart.

▶ You awake in a boat on the way to a large building that resembles a tree. Explore the room you awake in, and look through a window in a wooden door to see a rebel village. Turn to face the table. A woman, named Nelah, brings you Catherine's journal and your trap book. She mentions Catherine's name, although you cannot understand her language.

▶ Examine the journal. Note the entry about a pin that locks the telescope, and find a series of five D'ni numbers. Later, Nelah returns with a linking book. Touch the link image to return to the room with 25 stones.

▶ Leave the Moiety gateway tunnel. If the lights are out, keep clicking to get to the trap door. Pull the ring to exit. Turn right to the end of the catwalk and go down the ladder. Turn around and follow the catwalk into the cavern through the blue-lit cave, and past the jungle and clear-cut area. Return to the tram, which takes you back to Temple Island. Go through the Temple, up the passageway, and across the bridge to the Gate Room.

▶ Push the rotation button to set the doorways to Positions 1 and 3. Go to Position 3, where the ramp beyond now extends upward to a vertical slit high in the Great Golden Dome. Cross the ramp and enter a high, narrow passageway. Note a lever on the wall, and beyond, the Marble Puzzle.

▶ Look at the marble grid. Six marbles are lined up to the right. The grid is a five-by-five array of squares further divided into smaller squares, exactly like the array you saw in the Map Room on Plateau Island.

▶ Place colored marbles in the appropriate spots, based on what you learned in the Map Room and at the Color Wheel. The color is determined by the symbol that opened each dome. The positions are determined by consulting your notes from your session in the Map Room.

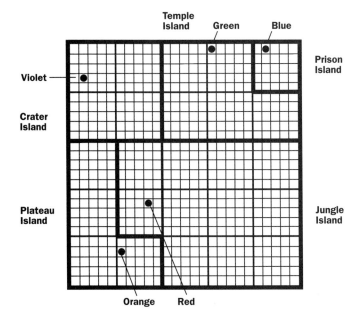

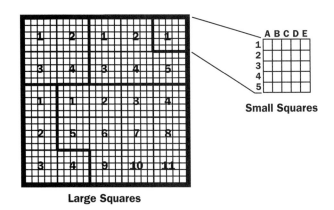

Large Squares

Small Squares

▶ When you think you have it right, step back and throw the switch on the wall. This lowers the marble press. Push the white button on the wall switch when it appears. An explosion and whooshing sound signals that the marbles are set correctly. You have now powered up the linking books in all of the Fire Marble Domes.

▶ If there is no whooshing sound, the marbles were positioned incorrectly, so try again. You must guess at one of the colors. Experiment until you get the right setting.

▶ Return to the Gate Room and go to Position 1. Press the rotation button three times to set the gates to Positions 1 and 4.

▶ Go through Position 4 and follow the catwalk beyond. Go into the Golden Dome. Turn left on the catwalk and cross the walkway extension. Pass the entrance to Position 3 in the Gate Room and go down the steps to the Golden Dome's lower level catwalk. Exit the door and follow the walkway to the right past the power valve for the West Drawbridge. Stop on a red plate on the path and turn right. Push the button to take the elevator down a level. Turn and follow the tunnel to some steps that lead up. Go up to the Fire Marble Dome.

▶ You now have the five numbers for the dome lock settings from Gehn's lab journal. Move the sliders to the appropriate numbers on the scale and push the button, opening the inner dome and raising the linking book. Open the book and touch the scene inside to travel to Gehn's universe.

Gehn's World

▶ You arrive inside a cage. Note the linking books, each with a graphic symbol of a different island. Turn until you see a button on a star-shaped design mounted on the bars. Touch it to call Gehn and have him talk to you. He talks about being trapped on Riven without books, but you know he has been writing books. He tells you that he is a changed man who wants to atone for the trouble he's caused.

▶ He also smokes frogs and wears a grand version of the uniform worn by the guard who first greeted you upon your arrival. You know that he uses the wahrks to instill fear in the natives, and—if the elaborate native warning network and Moiety rebellion are any indication—that the natives are, indeed, terrified of him. All suggest that Gehn is not to be trusted.

► He asks you to go through the trap book first, so he can satisfy himself that it is, indeed, a linking book to D'ni. When he holds the trap book in front of you, click on the picture and you'll get trapped inside the book. Watch while Gehn decides to follow you to D'ni. He gets trapped, which frees you, and you are now inside his home outside the cage.

► Find the switch that turns on the power to the other linking books in the room, and move it to the right.

► Find a lever next to a window, and pull it to lower the bars to your former cage.

► Find a tunnel leading down a ladder to Gehn's bedroom. Examine the various artifacts in the room. Go to the bedside table and examine his personal journal.

► Click on the gray metal sphere on the table, which appears to be some kind of watch. Listen to the sequence of sounds, which are the code to Catherine's prison.

► Go back up the ladder to the main room. Go into the cage area. There's a book that links to Prison Island here, the one with a single small square as an identifying graphic. Link to Catherine's island.

Catherine's Prison

► You arrive inside the Fire Marble Dome on Catherine's island. Press the button on the floor to the right of the book to lower the book stand and open the dome. Turn and follow the walkway toward a gigantic tree stump covering the entire small, rocky island. Go up the stairs and through a door to an elevator. Note three keys and a lever, plus a pull cord. Press the keys and listen to the different sounds. Enter the correct sequence of sounds (the sequence you heard on the watch in Gehn's bedroom), and then throw the lever to open the cage.

▶ Catherine joins you and pulls the elevator handle to descend. She congratulates you. "We're all free! You captured Gehn!" She tells you to open the fissure and reminds you that the combination is in her journal.

▶ Go back to Gehn's residence. You'll have to stop the dome again because Catherine has just used it.

End Game

▶ In Gehn's home, return to Temple Island by means of the Linking Book. Go through the tunnel to the elevator and press the button to take you up one level. Go through the Golden Dome to the Gate Room. Go through Position 1 and turn right, going down the stone steps.

▶ Return to the place where you first arrived on the island, at the telescope. Use the code from Catherine's journal to open the hatch. Look through the view finder to see stars in the fissure. Pull open the pin that blocks the telescope's descent by clicking on the support strut to the left of the hatch, and then swinging the lever handle up. Step back to the main controls and pull down the lever to the right of the scope. Press the green button.

▶ Repeatedly press the button until the glass breaks.

▶ Now watch Riven destroy itself. Atrus comes through from the chamber in which you first arrived on the island. Catherine arrives a moment later and they embrace; she tells you the villagers are all safely in the Rebel Age. "The path home is now clear for all of us."

▶ Atrus has brought a linking book. Catherine goes through to safety first. He then links through himself, letting the book fall into the fissure. You follow, falling into the Star Fissure… on your way home at last.

Riven: The Lost Episodes

With the help of this game guide, of course, you made it all the way through Riven without a single mistake or wrong turn. Want to see how the game ends if you don't perform so brilliantly?

Restore to a saved game made just *before* the final few moves of play.

You Fail to Trap Gehn

If you fail to trap Gehn before opening the Star Fissure, you lose the game. Atrus will arrive and ask you where Catherine and the book are. As a dawning horror appears on his face, he says, "I don't understand!"

"You never did!" cries Gehn, appearing behind him with a guard. At a signal from as the world crumbles, Atrus is killed by a blowgun dart.

Gehn retieves the Linking Book—his gateway back to D'ni and freedom—and then walks close to you, smiling. "I don't know what you thought you were doing," he says, vastly amused, "but… thank you!" Gesturing with the book, he adds, "I finallly am… free…

He then signals the guard, who shoots you with a blowgun dart.

You fall into darkness as a world dies.

You Fail to Free Catherine

If you trap Gehn but fail to free Catherine before smashing the glass view port in the Star Fissure, Atrus will come through and take the book. "I don't understand..." He looks at you, bewildered. "You've trapped Gehn, but... why did you signal me? There's no time left. The age is collapsing."

The shock and grief on his face when he realizes that Catherine may be lost forever should spur you on to return to the world of Riven again, this time to end the quest on a less tragic note.

For now, though, the wind howls as a world and a people die.

Make sure you both trap Gehn in the Book *and* release Catherine from her prison, using the code in Gehn's bedroom and you won't have to experience either of these unpleasant endings!

Good luck, and happy adventuring!

APPENDIX A
How It All Came To Be

Long ago, the great civilization of D'ni fell, wrecked by inner discords difficult for outsiders to comprehend. At the height of their power, however, the D'ni had ruled a thousand worlds, worlds that they had built with godlike power and linked to through the creation of their wondrous, half-magical books, a craft perfected by the D'ni across a span of ten thousand years.

Last of the D'ni was Gehn, a child when his world collapsed. When his young wife died years later, he left his newborn son in his mother's care and returned to D'ni's vast caverns and fallen cities. The art of making books and worlds had been lost with civilization's fall, but somehow he would learn the ancient secrets and restore lost D'ni.

For Gehn, it was clear that D'ni's glory could only be restored by the rediscovery of the lost craft of the books, a craft which he could learn only through the painstaking piecing together of scattered, subtle clues and bits of lore sifted from the subterranean ruins of D'ni's fallen, empty cities. Perhaps, in that disconsolate desolation, he went a little mad. Or, perhaps, it was the task he'd set for himself, learning how to write out the description of an entire world, line by line in the peculiarly precise and descriptive vocabularies of the D'ni tongue.

Creating entire worlds…

Eventually, Gehn returned for his son, and together they continued the exploration of D'ni. Atrus learned the craft of writing books from his father. More, he exhibited a talent for writing that far surpassed that of the older man. His rich description, his keen powers of logic and observation, the depth of his understanding and of his abilities to unleash the expressive, creative power of the D'ni script, unveiled worlds utterly beyond the ken of his father. Atrus never presumed to claim he was creating these worlds; nevertheless, it was true that his worlds endured while each of those opened by Gehn sooner or later collapsed.

So it was with the world, or *age* as these book-linked worlds were known, that Gehn called his Fifth Age… the world that would one day be known as Riven.

But it wasn't long before creative differences blossomed into deadly enmity dividing father from son. Atrus could not understand his father's parsimony of words, the cold and empty leanness of his descriptive passages, the editorial callousness that seemed, to Atrus, to all but guarantee each world's collapse. Worse, to Atrus's mind, was Gehn's overweening pride and ambition, which drove him to abandon whole ages and their innocent inhabitants. Gehn seemed obsessed with creating more and more worlds, discarding each in turn when it proved less than perfect. For him, these worlds and their populations were his creations, imperfect sketches to be discarded when they failed to meet his artistic vision. He was, after all, their god.

For Atrus, however, these ages were pre-existing worlds, their populations *people*, not failed experiments to be swept away with the rest of the rubbish when the day's work was done. Atrus had a personal interest in those people; his wife, Catherine, was from the Fifth Age. In Atrus's opinion, Gehn's books were merely means of linking to these new and pre-existing worlds and

modifying them. But it seemed that those worlds invaded by Gehn were inevitably and swiftly doomed by the descriptions he inserted within their creative matrices.

The Fifth Age—Gehn never bothered to name his creations, preferring instead to give them only cold numbers—was a promising world, but like Gehn's other efforts, the seeds of its destruction were planted within its heart. Together, Catherine and Atrus decided to stop Gehn's rape of the worlds, intending to arrange things so that Riven would become his prison.

Together, they managed to trap Gehn on Riven, confronting him at the Star Fissure, removing the last linking book out of that age by dropping it down that eldritch rift in time and space. Many of the local Rivenese witnessed that confrontation, when Catherine stepped into another world through a linking book, vanishing like a wraith, and Atrus hurled himself after the book down the fissure. Gehn was, indeed, trapped as Atrus and Catherine had planned.

As a result, the natives learned that Gehn was no god, that Atrus and Catherine had bested him and trapped him in that world. Unfortunately, they leaped to several other, less solid conclusions: Believing that Atrus was a god who had stripped Gehn of his power, that Catherine, a native of Riven, had been chosen by Atrus as his bride, and that she, herself, was transforming into a god who would one day rule Riven forever. From this series of revelations was born the Moiety, dissidents in rebellion against the oppressive and tyrannical rule of Gehn.

The Moiety survived at first in a vast system of interlinking caves beneath the surface of Riven. Eventually, and with Catherine's help when she returned to her native world, the Moiety was able to secure a burned book from Gehn's laboratory, and with this Catherine was able to write the rebels an age of their own, a safe refuge from the tyrant's predations. They adopted a kind of stylized dagger as their emblem; their introduction of these daggers, manufactured in the Moiety Age, puzzled Gehn when he realized that the materials could not be coming from Riven. Catherine, to her dismay, was nothing less than a savior figure, a goddess in her own right come to deliver her people.

The Moiety Age, accessed through secret caverns and by cunningly contrived puzzles, might one day prove to be the salvation of the Rivenese. Unfortunately, before she could carry her plans further, Catherine was captured by Gehn and imprisoned on a tiny island, a fragment of the much larger, original isle of Riven.

Gehn's meddlings were taking their toll, and Riven was disintegrating faster and ever faster. Worse, perhaps, Gehn's tinkering had also changed the infrastructure of Riven to the extent that he could introduce certain key ingredients for his use. For example, a particular species of beetle that provided the necessary dyes for ink, a special type of tree whose pulped wood made paper of the proper fineness, tooth, and texture. He'd written all he needed into Riven; it seemed to enable him to continue his research into creating his own linking books. It took him thirty years, but eventually he did it. After hundreds of trials, after hundreds of failures, Gehn succeeded in creating a new world—his 233rd age—a haven from which he could complete his experiments.

Soon he would be free of crumbling Riven forever.

Atrus, meanwhile, was beset with the problem of what to do about Gehn. Fearing that Catherine was lost on Riven, he could not simply return to that age with a linking book, not if that meant that Gehn might seize the book and use it to effect his own escape. He feared, too, the imminent breakup of Riven, which was accelerating. His efforts were dangerously delayed by the rebellion of his sons, Achenar and Sirrus, in the Myst affair. Carried away by megalomania and greed (had they been touched by the disease of Atrus's father as well?), they trapped Atrus in D'ni, leaving him helpless, save for the writings with which he could implement certain changes in dying Riven.

Working furiously for many months, he managed to write those changes into Riven's matrix, slowing the destruction, but he knew with cold certainty that the final Armageddon of that age could not be long deferred. He could not observe the changes directly from his prison within D'ni, but he could note them on a fundamental level and understand that there was now no way the decay could ever be reversed. Catherine might well be doomed, and all of the inhabitants of Riven as well.

And then... a miracle. Someone, a stranger from another world, another *reality* beyond the Star Fissure, found the lost Myst book, used it to go through to the Isle of Myst, and, ultimately, managed to free Atrus from his prison on D'ni. The stranger seemed willing to help with the problem of Riven, although what he was being asked to do was extraordinarily dangerous.

Atrus would send the stranger into Riven carrying only a specially designed trap book, one that would appear to be a linking book back to D'ni. Atrus knew that Gehn could scarcely resist such a temptation—a means of escaping from Riven once and for all! Once the stranger had trapped Gehn, he would send a signal which would summon Atrus, bringing a real linking book to D'ni.

The stranger agreed.

And with this acceptance began the final chapter of the saga of Riven.

APPENDIX B
Worlds For The Making

An infinity of worlds… literally, worlds without end.

This is the promise of Riven, where books describing worlds create links to alternate realities, places, worlds, *ages* where people and life and even physical laws might be quite different than the mundane reality we know as Earth.

Purest fantasy, of course.

Or… is it?

Since the end of the nineteenth century, physics—the means by which we apprehend the cosmos and the laws that govern it—has been undergoing revolution upon stunning revolution, until all that is clear is J.B.S. Haldane's maxim that the universe is not only stranger than we imagine, it is stranger than we *can* imagine. That peculiarly twisty pocket of physics known as quantum mechanics arose from the discovery of the dual nature of light, packets of energy, or *quanta*, that can at one and the same time behave both as electromagnetic waves and as discrete particles. Physicist Werner Heisenberg went from there to the formulation of what came to be known as Heisenberg's Uncertainty Principle, which states that it is impossible to know both the position and the momentum of a subatomic particle without changing one or the other. In fact, the introduction of observation changes the very phenomena under observation; this so-called observer effect predicts that we help shape the universe simply by living here.

Such arrogance! To actually suggest that the existence of the universe, born of the "Big Bang" Theory billions of years before life or worlds evolved from its fires of energy and chaos, is dependent on the minds of humans or others to somehow will it into being smacks of nothing so much as a kind of megalomaniacal hubris, an arrogant, doomed assumption by Man of the prerogatives of God.

And yet, this seems to be precisely the way things work, as validated both by the mathematics of quantum mechanics, and by experimental results.

Erwin Schroedinger illuminated this radical, seemingly mystical notion by inventing a thought experiment, a well-known physical parable that today bears the name Schroedinger's Cat. Suppose, the parable goes, an experimenter places a live cat in a sealed box. With the cat is a vial of prussic acid, designed to be broken if and only if some random event—say, the decay of a given radioactive particle with a half-life of one hour—occurs.

The cat has a fifty-fifty chance of surviving the hour. At the end of sixty minutes, the experimenter opens the box. Will he find a live cat... or a dead one? More to the point, is the cat alive or dead *before the experimenter opens the box*?

According to one of the weirder interpretations of quantum theory, the correct answer is "yes." Until the box is open, say the equations, and the so-called "observer effect" comes into play, the cat is both alive and dead, a kind of mathematical wave function that does not, that *cannot*, collapse into one probability or the other until the cat's state is actually observed.

The discussion seems to fly in the face of reason. However, though this would hardly be the first time that insights into the way the universe works seemed to defy common sense. In fact, enough experimental evidence has accumulated since Heisenberg's day to suggest that quantum physics does, in fact, provide the best interpretation of how the universe—or the *universes*—actually work. One explanation—known as the Copenhagen Interpretation—postulates that every time a quantum event occurs (an electron goes up an energy level, its spin changes, it loses energy), a new universe branches off to accommodate the change.

This theory is controversial to say the least. Can it be that a new universe is born *each and every time* something as insubstantial as a photon is born, or the spin-state of an electron changes?

Perhaps nature is not so profligate. Perhaps the multiplicity of universes overlap somehow, in ways we cannot yet understand. Perhaps such overlappings explain how people could unknowingly step from one world to another, as seems to have happened upon occasion. The accounts of Charles Forte and of other books are filled with the names and descriptions of mysterious vanishings and arrivals—Kaspar Hauser, Judge Crater, the two women at the Garden of Triannon, the green children of Suffolk, the crew of the Marie Celeste, the ubiquitous "Grays" who *could* be extraterrestrial but who can exhibit powers more easily explained by extradimensional origins—and so very many more.

Even so, it seems that nothing less than an infinity of parallel universes, alternate realities distinct from one another yet ever splitting one from another like the branches of a tree, could embrace so bizarre a concept.

Infinity is a very *large* number, one that means that *anything* is possible—somewhere. An infinity of universes means that somewhere, somehow, every possible event or combination of events has taken place. Every alternate history ever imagined, every world of fantasy ever dreamed of, every universe conceived by every writer of science fiction, every hallucination spawned by every madman, all, *all* have concrete reality, somewhere. Did they exist from the beginning, or were they somehow created by the very act of thinking about them? The question may well be meaningless; time may be an illusion from the unique perspective of the metacosmos, and reality may require no more than *belief* to give it substance.

The Nobel-winning physicist Niels Bohr once commented, "Those who are not shocked when they first come across quantum theory cannot possibly have understood it."

In Riven, of course, the ancient D'ni learned to write books—using special papers, special inks, even a special and highly descriptive language—that allowed adepts among the people to cross over to other worlds. Or were they, in fact, creating those worlds? The concept hangs upon the space-twisting horns of the Copenhagen Interpretation.

And more…

Consider. Within the framework of quantum physics and the Worlds of If, it is quite possible—more, it is certain—that somewhere, some*when*, universes exist—infinities of them, in fact, where magic works. Where Sauron's minions seek the One Ring, and hobbits shun such inconvenient things as adventures. Where the Lensman battles the evil forces of dark Eddore, or where crystal cities gleam along the banks of the Grand Canal on Mars. Where Vikings colonized all of North America, or perhaps where the cause of Southern Independence was won at Gettysburg. Where *you* are president of the United States of Columbia… or Emperor of the Earth and all her far-flung colonies.

And worlds exist where books link world to world, where imagination creates entire ages, where the surface tension of water enables it to be sculpted like clay, where Catherine and Atrus struggle to stop the final collapse of Riven.

And where *you* arrive on a small and rocky island to find the fate of the Riven Age in your hands…

Temple Island

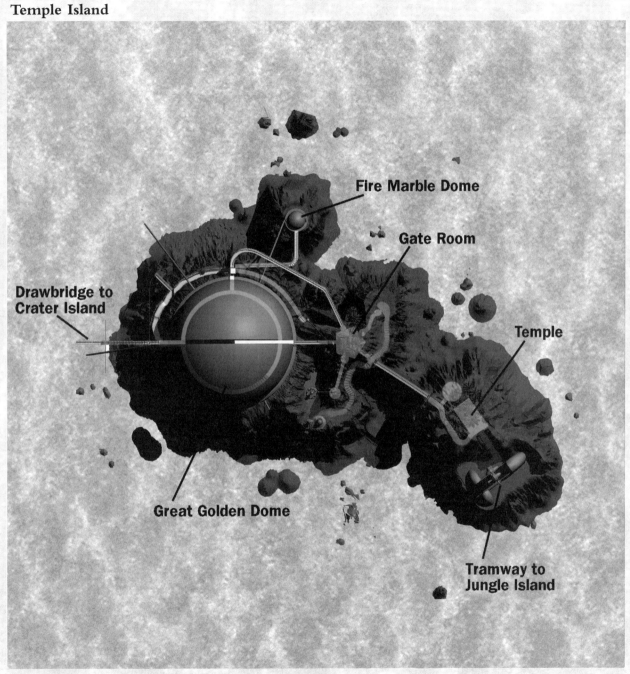

Fire Marble Dome

Gate Room

Drawbridge to
Crater Island

Temple

Great Golden Dome

Tramway to
Jungle Island

Jungle Island

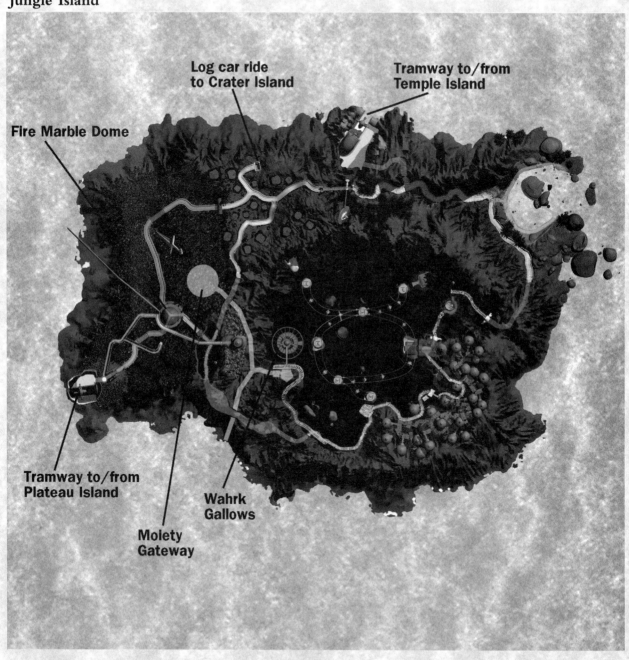

Log car ride
to Crater Island

Tramway to/from
Temple Island

Fire Marble Dome

Tramway to/from
Plateau Island

Wahrk
Gallows

Molety
Gateway

Plateau Island

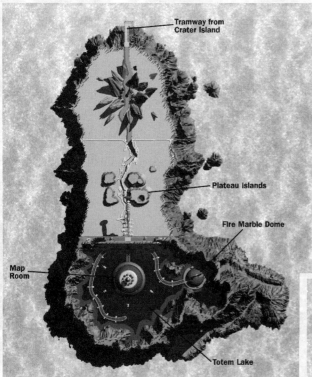

Tramway from
Crater Island

Plateau islands

Fire Marble Dome

Map
Room

Totem Lake

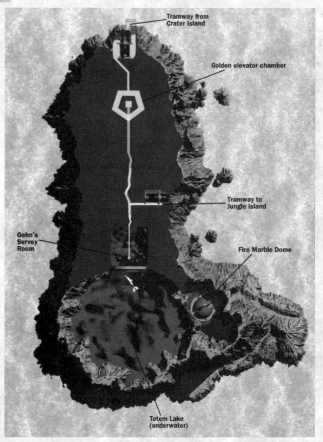

Tramway from
Crater Island

Golden elevator chamber

Tramway to
Jungle Island

Gehn's
Survey
Room

Fire Marble Dome

Totem Lake
(underwater)

Crater Island

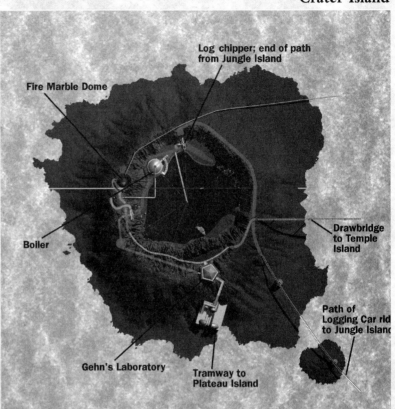

Log chipper; end of path from Jungle Island

Fire Marble Dome

Boiler

Drawbridge to Temple Island

Path of Logging Car rid to Jungle Island

Gehn's Laboratory

Tramway to Plateau Island

Prison Island

Fire Marble Dome

Catherine's Prison

High above Temple Island, we see the exact arrival location for anyone linking to Riven.

A richly adorned
location for Gehn
and his ministers
in addition to
being an access
hub to various
locations on
the island.

Here, Gehn's
most monumen-
tal architectural
effort, foreshad-
ows most of this
rocky island.

Transport between the surface and underground survey room is accomplished by using this subterranean elevator.

This Magnetic Levitation Car, suspended on an electromagnetic "cushion," provides quick transportation between the islands. Gehn used flexible cables as a means of compensating for the islands' gradual movement apart.

The lower plateau, shown here, is one of the areas Gehn has stripped, reshaped, and reformed to proclaim his power over nature.

The pulp boiler as seen from the crater's lake.

Close-up of the various levers, wheels, and gauges of Gehn's pulp boiler.

Using the scopes
flanking each
side of his chair
high atop a flight
of stairs, Gehn
can observe the
entire island and
his prisoner,
Catherine.

Pathway to the lagoon. A favorite gathering spot for the often seen, but cautious, baleened animals.

The native villagers built these suspended adobe "cliff dwellings" within the crater of this island.

Here in the school room, we see a close-up of Gehn's imager (center) and the students' lesson in D'ni (on the left).

The spherical watch seen here was a gift from Gehn's mother, Anna.

This close-up view of Gehn's desk reveals his precise nature.

Within Gehn's office resting high atop the heavily eroded spires in Gehn's Age, we see a view past his desk (center) to the eerie, caustic afternoon sky.

Atop the massive remnant of the great tree,
its roots still buried deep beneath the water's
surface, rests a small building.